SOLUM JOURNAL
VOLUME IV

SOLUM JOURNAL
VOLUME IV

AN IMPRINT OF SOLUM LITERARY PRESS

Solum Journal is a biannual literary journal. It is a project of Solum Literary Press, a Christian small press publishing poetry, fiction, homilies, and visual art.

MASTHEAD

Riley Bounds, Publisher and Editor in Chief
Christine Pelliccio, Managing Editor and Visual Art Editor
Douglas J. Lindquist, Content Editor and Theology Editor
Matthew J. Andrews, Poetry Editor
Laura Reece Hogan, Associate Poetry Editor
Ryan Rickrode, Fiction Editor
Elizabeth Genovise, Associate Fiction Editor
Sarah Christolini, Graphic Designer
Emma Winchell, Social Media Editor

SOLUM LITERARY PRESS

15850 N Thompson Peak Pkwy, 2176

Scottsdale, AZ 85260

(480) 371-9053
info@solumpress.com

For submission guidelines, purchasing, and subscription information, please visit https://www.solumpress.com.

CONTENTS

EDITOR'S NOTE

During this volume's production, my father died unexpectedly. In reviewing the material for this issue, I noticed a sizable amount of submissions centering around grief, or at the very least somber reflection. This was organic; we hadn't requested themed submissions. As such, it seemed fitting to dedicate this volume to the themes of lament, loss, and doubt from a Christian perspective. Normally, I wouldn't feature my own work in Solum, but I've made an exception here, including a trilogy of previously-published poems in honor of my father.

Brothers and sisters in Christ frequently point to the lament psalms for those grieving. It's often said they always end in hope. But not all do. Some end in unanswered pleas (Ps. 44, 74, 80, 88). In the whirlwind, God displayed power to Job, not answers (Job 38–41). When Lazarus died, Jesus didn't offer Mary a sermon or remind her that he wasn't in pain anymore. Jesus wept (John 11:32–35). Similarly, the pieces in this volume don't always neatly resolve. They don't always end in hopeful exhortations. Many end in silence. Silence is the sound of God listening.

This issue is dedicated to Gayle Bounds.

Lie you easy, dream you light,
And sleep you fast for aye;
And luckier may you find the night
Than ever you found the day.
- A. E. Housman, "The Isle of Portland"

CALL TO LAMENT

KAT HAYES

Miserere

Oh unfathomed God, you perceive this tempest.
How it looks in your timeless view of time,
I cannot say. Eons might elapse in a beat–
a specter of breath slipping from glass.
My offerings are nothing you need,
still I struggle and bargain against pain.
From here, the losses are too often beyond
reason, beyond enumeration. What strange math
holds everything in your boundless mind–
cicada, kestrel, trillium, strand of hair?
What grave mystery makes a gift of your silence?
For today, make this my offering–
Just this morning, winds from a world away
swept clouds across the sun. I stood in the light,
and the dark, and the light.

Kat Hayes is Assistant Professor of English at Eastern University near Philadelphia. Her writing has been published or is forthcoming in several print and online publications including Black Lawrence Press, *Ecotone, Cimarron Review, Salamander, Ruminate, Nimrod*, and *Off the Coast*. She and her husband have two spirited daughters and two somnolent cats.

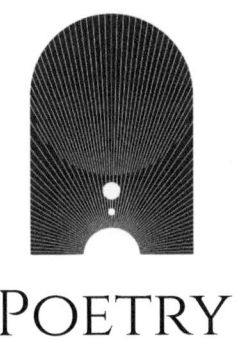

POETRY

Timothy E. G. Bartel

Dizain for the Dormition

She died. That is the lore passed down to us
from those who knew her. Unlike Him, she did
grow old and slow, stood still, and made a fuss
about some little trifle, less to rid
herself of petty anger than to bid
the men to be more patient. There is worth
in hurry to evangelize the earth,
but not quite yet, when she is still right there,
her blue and simple dress, the tale of birth
that she repeats, sometimes, to empty air.

Dizain for Joan Didion

What you have done to sentences,
the California hills have done
to you. We are apprentices
still guided by the western sun
to shape a clause, to clean a gun,
to think of murder, truth, and home
beneath the star-pricked velvet dome
of lonely nights in Riverside.
Your death has cast a lasting gloam
on language—we crusade, elide.

Timothy E. G. Bartel is a poet and professor from California. His poems have appeared in *Christianity and Literature*, *First Things*, *Solum Journal*, and elsewhere. His latest book of poems is *A Crown for Abba Moses: New and Selected Poems* (Solum, 2023), and his new book of critical essays, *The Poets and the Fathers*, is forthcoming from Pickwick Publications. Timothy currently lives and teaches in Houston.

Laura R. McCullough

Hope Is Like a Bird
or Two Stones

I.
At the death of distance,
we found them together.
Elbows touching
at the kitchen
table cleaned
last for my father and first
for this missing
person; their artifact a trail
of little black and white
squares.

In albums we found them
hiding from life
with the people in them,
gray icons of a world
sure it had always existed.

I knew better.

This history that would
betray the gaps
by filling them
was cast with characters from
someone else's story.

How could my life be
shaped so
by a woman
hiding in plain sight?
Shreds of what I could touch,

pattern paper and unfinished
curtain hems;
the outline of a person
somehow enough to set
my moorings,
yet not able to bear
any weight.

In some battles the only
survivor is the fear
of everything.

This woman who
was a mountain,
crossed lines and stitches,
wires and oceans,
who could never
bring herself to teach
me anything that
might hurt.
Could never bring up
the hurting already there.

She was a whole continent to me.
Afternoons and decades
given to places
no one has ever really been.

Bargains made with God
come up lost in the winning.

The smell of her on the couch,
to a child, was never
the smell of an unwashed body,
or of spark and wit
turned
to a spiraling self-neglect.

Spiraling like endless
apple peels
skinned for pies that said
I love you
when no one knew the words.
It was never the smell of
isolation.

It was just
her.

II.
All the beauty in the world
lived in her mother; fading
here in gelatin and silver.
The after made her angry,
hard in the buried places
and settled with bitterness.

The warmth and wonder
held in smooth hands,
the longing in her voice
when she spoke
of anywhere but here;
all calendar pages and
clipped wings.

With Saints and
mortars blurred in the
thunder, no one
can play in the rain.

Hope fossilized
in linoleum
is too brittle an anchor
for much footing

this side of the Wall.
The stories she chose
for me to know her,
scattered coins,
never enough together
to buy a meal.
So much less *her*
than the smell of the couch.

Fear of wasting
and wanting
steeped into the spine of the house,
pressing your weak points
so that you would be strong,
more than they were,
better.

For all the birds
we could not eat, and
the bones that wouldn't scrape clean,
she gave me only and all
the parts of herself that could
stand the sunlight.
But I don't think we ever
wanted to be better;
only to be
whole.

Intersection

We walked for miles
asking the wrong questions,
our feet finding truth
in the pavement.

Hard eyes sliding off
like raindrops the summer heat
refused us, while a raw gaze
more human than my sliding
               pace
appraised the wear on my shoes.

There is space for footsteps and
               breath
                    between
the buildings and the people; a whispered
prayer misjudged the distance. Worth

is a presence, not a product.

In my bag full of smooth
ideas, I took home a stone.

I can't say if the worn face,
the salt and weariness of it,
held a shred of hope in his eyes.

I did not look. I kept walking.
Made altars of the sidewalk and
pressed into the other
side of my vision, said
               something
                    sounding
important; I want to go back.

Tell him he was seen. Overturn
tables and expectations, be equity
to the invisible.

The gray. To change
          more
lives than my own. But the truth is
I would not have walked here

alone. The parking ticket,
humbling me while serving
as the price for admission.

Before I saw the little bee
                    dragging
                              down
the gutter, outmatched
by scouts bringing
          home
a meal, the measure
of steps and connection had been
scale enough for the street.

As thoughts dug in like
the ants clamoring
over their victory,

too much for them to haul,
pieces of pieces
          lost
on the way, I
could still see the bee.

Even in his pieces, he held

the whole burden of the day.

Poured out and sojourning
on streets with no flowers.
Vibrating against failure
his wings, built for the sunlight,

feeding
           nothing
                    now.
His captors not knowing he dies
for them. *He died* for them.

Tasting my own debt,
had I paid what was
           owed
to the man hawking roses,
I could have saved two lives.

Laura R. McCullough is an artist and writer happily nestled with her family in the North Georgia mountains. A "lover of faith and believer in what is beautiful," she and her husband minister through their testimony of healing to help bring light to others. Laura uses her writing and mark-making to explore how deep wounds can make room for the deepest roots. Her work has been published in journals such as *Rattle Magazine*, *The Blue Mountain Review*, and *Right Angle*, and her artwork is featured in several regional museums and galleries. Some of her work and thoughts can be found at speakyoursouldesign.com and Instagram @speakyoursoulpage.

SARAH B. CAHALAN

He asked me to throw him in the water

but I'm afraid he's still sitting on a shelf.
As my father died, he drifted
in and out of believing — sometimes
storm surge, sometimes drought.
I had hoped to inter him more traditionally.
I called Our Lady of the Cape all the way
from Ohio, so Fr. would pay him
a visit. You have to catch the wave just right,
as lifesavers launching surfboats know.
Waves come in threes. In fact he raged
at the priest and also everything. I confess:
I was proud of his honesty. Nevertheless
(and this is where I cross myself) later
he saw a woman through his suffering —
I would never lie about this — a mother.
A mother called him over (though perhaps
it was the morphine drip).
Which mother? His? I'm sure
I can't say for certain.
But it's in the medical records I have kept
with his urn, his watch, with his logbooks
in which he recorded sailing to the wreck,
to the creek, to the deep-dark places
where bay gives way to ocean.

Roadside

The deer that died on the highway
lodged its broken body in my son's heart.

It was there after therapy on Friday but
by Monday, gone.

Now every time we pass that spot
he asks how it is doing, is it better,

Should we call the doctor? He asks after
the deer long-disposed-of by scavengers,

by the department of transportation,
by the elements of the middle Midwest.

The truth is, I don't know how the deer
is doing or where it is,

whether its antlers rest on a mossy bed
in the green light of the gloaming,

in a forest free of predators,
of the no-oh-no of an approaching car.

The deer is gone but you can still address it.
Driving past graveyards, now,

intoning "rest in peace, deer,"
we speak its new creation into existence

together. Words hard-won.
Love branching out of his little self.

Sarah B. Cahalan writes about art, books, faith, natural history, the layers of places and how those correspond with our own layers as people moving through time and place. She has poems, current or forthcoming, in *The Shore*; *the tide rises, the tide falls*; *Skipjack Review*; *The Milton Review*; and *U. S. Catholic*. Sarah is based in Dayton, Ohio.

Riley Bounds

Father.

You didn't
call me
about the
rapture
today.
Twenty-six years
of any day
now,
how everyone
would
pay,
and I don't
know
how to tell
you
I don't
think
God will save
us
from what's
already
happened.
But rant,
shout,
break your voice
against my
head
and let me

Originally published in *Adelaide Literary Award 2019 Poetry Anthology*, edited by Stevan
Nikolic, Adelaide Books, 2019, 292-294.

hear it,
because I'd rather
shiver in
your noise
than stand in
your silence.
Your heart
was always
a war
drum.
So stay
and tithe
your noise.
Stay,
and maybe
one day
gravity will
reverse,
all our ash
will fall
up,
and all the world's
fires
will spiral
into the upper
atmospheres
like jet
streams,
and all
that'll be
left
on the ground
is
what's
pure.
All our traumas
happened while

the sky watched,
so let's give it
hell,
let's give it
a taste,
you and
me,
whatever gives you
war,
whatever keeps you
fighting.
Keep
your dogs
this side
of memory.
Keep watching
for pale horses
and holes
in the sky,
listen for
the eagle,
just don't
stop
talking.

Father, Again.

Dreamed we
stamped out fires
in a smoldering
home.
You told me
you were proud
of my tribulation
heart,
just don't trust
every one that's
bled.
Hugged me
as our dead dog
bayed outside,
and then I woke
to the truths
whispering in
my ceiling.

Originally published in *Ekstasis Magazine* Issue 07, edited by Conor Sweetman, *Ekstasis Magazine*, 2020, 29–30.

Father, Forever.

Sun burned bright in you the 30 years you gave me. Falling star down the road, 90 miles an hour in 30 zones. Flame trails caught the trees, spread. We are not so cosmic. We aren't meant to hold the heat, keep everything in balance. Plasma become flare, you become hell. But hell isn't a one-man tomb. Thirty years shed. Face in your cinder.

In the world you've consumed, I remember the ones you created. The ones in oil pastel and sketch paper. The ones told to me in my racecar bed before sleep. The ones we made in the log rides at the state fair and the carousel afterwards. I remember the dogs we've buried, the houses we built, the walks down wood paths only we knew. These are the worlds you burned for. Those are the worlds you've become. Son to father, father to sun, sun in the Son.

I'll miss you forever, Dad.

— son

In memory of Gayle Bounds, February 27th, 1955 – September 7th, 2023

Originally published in *Ekstasis Magazine*, edited by Conor Sweetman, *Ekstasis Magazine*, https://www.ekstasismagazine.com/poetry/2023/father-forever.

Riley Bounds is Publisher and Editor in Chief of Solum Literary Press. He holds an MA in Philosophy from Talbot School of Theology at Biola University and a BA in Creative Writing from the University of Central Oklahoma. He is a poet and fiction writer. A 2021 Pushcart Prize nominee, his work has appeared or is forthcoming in *The Windhover*, *Presence*: *A Journal of Catholic Poetry*, *Earth and Altar*, *Ekstasis Magazine*, *Amethyst Review*, and *Heart of Flesh Literary Journal*, among others. His debut chapbook, *Hands of Years,* was released by Kelsay Books in 2021. He teaches humanities and journalism at Arizona Christian University and writes for *The Center That Holds* blog on Patheos.

Kat Hayes

Skunk Hollow

After we were broken irreparably,
I went to the creek. I was always going
To creeks in the face of loss as if things
Might be mended there by geology.

Except I had no sense of place. I might
Have started with the remains of a mill
Nearby, three hundred years old and still.
No water bringing the wheel to life,

No wheat abraded by the pair of stones–
They lay in the sun turned upward like eyes.
The mill stood indifferent to time while
I tried to make sense of being alone.

I was trying to parse how we split
Like two limbs of a tree. I got nowhere.
Like sound, the blame ricocheted here, there–
Yes, we were hollow. Yes, we were careless.

It took time for me to get my bearings,
But I kept coming back to this– the mill,
The creek, the stones kept apart by skill
Or luck, the wheel causing water to sing.

In theory, we could still go back and revise
the story: I gave you what I was able.
What you took from me was a miller's toll–
the portion of bread that kept you alive.

Kat Hayes is Assistant Professor of English at Eastern University near Philadelphia. Her writing has been published or is forthcoming in several print and online publications including Black Lawrence Press, *Ecotone, Cimarron Review, Salamander, Ruminate, Nimrod,* and *Off the Coast.* She and her husband have two spirited daughters and two somnolent cats.

CAMERON BROOKS

Prairie Archipelago

They say some ancient glacier is to blame
for this — a flooded farmhouse, a gaunt silo
rising from a nameless lake. We drift by

in silence, casting our lines around the rubble,
permitting the wind to carry us where it carries
all things: whitecaps and walleye, three pelicans

squatting at shore beside a shot tractor tire.
Why have we come here? To fish, of course,
and to savor the contingency of being

between bites; to wait wondering at the old
highway that plunges into the lake; to watch
thick thunderheads descending from the north.

Antique Store, Somewhere, South Dakota

A fading portrait of a stoic tribal chieftain
in his feathered headdress, sitting a horse.
A corner for a shoddy chestnut saddle
and other equestrian tack: leather boots,
ten pair, a bucket of spurs, thin lariats
strung around the pommel. Wide-brim hats,
of course, with beaded drawstrings for riding
in the wind. Reams of vintage postcards:
Mt. Rushmore, Fort Collins, St. Paul.
Next, stacks of rusty license plates for every
state west of Missouri. Ten dollars each.
Glass cases of curios: phantom keys,
pocket knives, Zippo lighters, dead
wrist watches, other nameless trinkets.
Embroidered dish towels, Larimar jewelry.
Spoons. Magazine clippings of slim house-
wives tilted in their aprons, advertising
kitchenware. A colossal bison head
trophy-mount, protruding from the wall.
Racks of double-barrel rifles and crimson
Navajo print rugs and hundreds of
growlers, bottles, jars, cans, and mugs.
One glossy green ashtray from Vegas.
Some cowboy poetry. In the far back,
a dark woodcut profile of a familiar man,
stuck with a red sale sticker: "Jesus."
His beard gathers dust; cheap gods don't sell.

Cameron Brooks is an MFA candidate at Seattle Pacific University. His work is found or forthcoming in *Poetry East*, *Third Wednesday*, *North Dakota Quarterly*, *Pasque Petals*, *Ad Fontes Journal*, and elsewhere. Cameron lives in Sioux Falls, South Dakota. Instagram: @camerondbrooks.

SARAH TATE

Peace, Lord

It is dark, it is silent, here
in land apart from real land,
where the stars, now, they are
bits of bone in the soil.
I hope, and I fear, running hands
over the white seed of the moon,
teeth shiny, light like crunched glass,
glittering, because the Earth still turns—
its blood is rough honey flowing from a rock,
but listen, for its whispers
are twitches of eternal muscles,
heartbeats of shine-blind holy things.

Mercy for those who live in time.
Soft touches across our cold,
broken jaws, crushed eyes, dead ones.
Peace, Lord, for us who must
bear the bruises of twilight.
We are temporary immortals.
Look now, the sun rises, spring-time
peach and pink, as though light is forever,
as deep as awe, golden and new.
Lord, take the sky from my hands
while the wonder parades
through the flowers of the garden.

Wednesday's Ash

Hooked rug covered
with upturned sunlight.
Blots like the butts
of cigarettes,
brown floorboards wet
with the verge of June.

Three slanting trees
weighed low by the noon,
myrtles near the fences.
Just seen, as long as
forever is, by the light
of the late afternoon.

The music of a cello
floats along the heads
of graves. It will be
the same grief flying
when peonies sprout
beneath the names.

Rows of dawn fan out,
collect like coins
in the offering plate.
Here, there, wistful we
are, always, for a new
and different world.

Sarah Tate is a poet and writer from Partlow, Virginia, where she enjoys taking long walks by the trees and reading good books on the porch. Her work often meditates on the embodied world, eternal reflections, and the intersection between philosophy and ordinary life. Currently, she is pursuing a master's degree in English from Liberty University, where she is also an editor and contributor for the literary press *LAMP*. Besides *Solum*, her work has been featured in *Amethyst Review*, *Calla Press*, *Heart of Flesh*, and elsewhere.

LAURA E. LUCHT

Tending Leyla

The bedpan and the high-heeled shoe
commiserate on the worn parquet.
Eight beds fill this ward, sixteen living souls:
the wounded and those who tend them.

Smell the greasy chicken soup, iodine, and sweat.
Shuffle wooden chairs for nightly vigils.
The surgeon drones through teatime rounds.
A grizzled woman snoozes in her body cast.
Her niece knits socks from crimson wool.

Last night, while Leyla slept, the woman
in the next bed retched as orderlies
shouted and threaded a tube down her throat.
I watched the Angel of Death
pace the courtyard beneath
our second-story window.

Baku, Azerbaijan

Laura E. Lucht grew up in the Sierra Nevada mountains of California and currently resides near Seattle, Washington, where she is an M.F.A. candidate in Creative Writing at Seattle Pacific University. She holds an M.A. International Studies from the University of Washington and a B.A. in Russian & Soviet Studies and Linguistics from UC San Diego. In her free time, she goes for walks in the woods and chases rabbits out of her tiny garden.

SALLY THOMAS

In The Courtyard

A coal fire thrummed and murmured on the darkness.
Its shiver lit a crowd of human faces,
Cold-pinched and dirtied by its licking shadow,
And by their hungry waiting for the something
About to happen that was bound to happen.
Behind the heavy doors, the hidden voices —
No one outside could hear what they were saying,
But only how they rose and fell. The stranger
Who warmed his hands among them tuned his hearing
For that one voice he would have recognized.

He listened, too, within himself, half-hoping
To find, again, some echo of his own voice,
Exhorting — something — in the mountain starlight,
Mere days ago. Or centuries. He'd thought, then,
That heaven would ignite its temple fire,
And all the earth would rise on wings of incense,
While prophets spoke with prophets in bright shadow,
A shuddering of glory. *Tell no one.*

Tonight he felt he dreamed these faces, voices.
The wrong firelight kept flickering through gardens,
This most wrong garden, filled with such wrong faces —
No one familiar, only a confusion
Of avid voices fastened on him, asking.
What could he think to say? *I do not know him.*
That clarity had been his. All that vision.
Now — startled, in the dark — he told no one.

Hunters in the Snow

After Pieter Brueghel the Elder

These distances have frozen. In a field,
Ice the river left has trapped the sky.
Trees look down at it. The scene revealed
Through afternoon's blue scrim makes no reply

To men returning, weary, with their kill.
No one is singing now. Even the crow
Hanging on the air says nothing. Hill,
Black naked branch, late winter's deadened snow

Afraid to trust the world with its cold weight:
No one is singing. Christmastime is past.
On the pond, the small black figures skate
Beneath a murky sky. The furnace-blast

Of inn-yard fire — more figures, roasting corn —
Has knocked the sign askew. Or something has.
Wind, or time. Saint Hubert, all forlorn
In smoke and gold-leaf halo, trains his gaze

On empty woods. The deer have run away.
No one is singing. Bearing home one hare,
These men, these slinking dogs, regret the day.
The snow melts underfoot, refreezes there.

Sally Thomas is the author of two poetry collections: *Motherland*, which was a finalist for the Able Muse Book Award, and *Among the Living*, also from Able Muse Press, forthcoming in 2024. Her debut novel, *Works of Mercy*, appeared from Wiseblood Books in 2022. She is co-editor of the Paraclete Press anthology *Christian Poetry in America Since 1940*, which received the 2023 Book Award in Culture and the Arts from *Christianity Today*. As associate poetry editor for the *New York Sun*, she shares the writing of a weekday Poem of the Day column. The mother of four grown children, she lives with her husband and dog in North Carolina.

TOMMY WELTY

Emmaus

Will we all race in some mad crash
to the finish? Or, meander to the end
when every beautiful thing is ash,

having ignored the sword caught in the latch,
the finger pointing east to send
us racing? Let madness crash

across your heart, this storm gnash
its teeth against you. Rend
everything beautiful, burn it all to ash.

Stranger, stay with us. Unlash
us from what we carry, lend
us wisdom of the maddening crash

of suffering and glory. Eyes flash
and we see the hand of a friend.
Ask: Did our hearts not race madly? Crash
and burn within us, finding only beautiful things in ash?

Tommy Welty is a poet and pastor in Southern California where he lives with his wife and children. His poetry has appeared in *Ekstasis*, *The Windhover*, *Heart of Flesh Literary Journal*, and others.

PATRICK CABELLO HANSEL

It Had Ceased to Be with Sarah After the Manner of Women

No candlestick. No cool
cloth over my head at the heat
of the day. Still the sifting,
the stirring, the pounding
of the heel of my hand on
the masa to make the loaves.
Bread that does not fill.
Cavern ever empty, only a sore
like a cistern dripping water.
I kept a chest with precious
stones gathered on our journeys:
turquoise, lapis lazuli,
a stinging insect caught in amber.
Bones, now. Splinters of limbs
that never grew. Yes, I laughed.
The laugh of bitterness wearied
by holding sorrows at arm's lengths
all these barren years. My time
now reduced to "after": after
I have grown old; after my husband
is good as dead, shall I have pleasure?
Shall we? I have a choice to make
with my one, tried body: I can rise
up in joy, I can grasp this promise
one more season; or I can fold
my flesh into a rock. I can
lie down. I can cease.

Another Day Another Funeral

The freshly washed
and pressed pall

casts a shadow,
not on the coffin

nor the mourners
huddled in groups

of two, seven, one,
but on the high

arch of the old church
where chipped paint

hangs bravely silent.
Years of votive soot

cling to each flake
like forgotten sins

waiting to float down
on the faithful

and absolve them,
not because

they have repented
fully, or in part,

but because God
has surrendered —

the flakes are God's
and the sins that cling.

We do not look up
to capture the falling;

we are all shadows,
casting our lives

into a vast sea,
hoping to be caught.

Patrick Cabello Hansel is a poet and retired Lutheran pastor, who served for 35 years in urban, bilingual congregations in the Bronx, Philadelphia, and Minneapolis. His poetry collections are _The Devouring Land_ (Main Street Rag Publishing), _Quitting Time_ (Atmosphere Press), and _Breathing in Minneapolis_ (Finishing Line Press), which deals with the challenges that city faced in the past three years. He has published poems and prose in over 85 journals and won awards from the Loft Literary Center and MN State Arts Board. He is currently working on a novel, as well as serializing his second novella in a local newspaper. His website is www. artecabellohansel.com.

CARLA GALDO

Elegy for All Souls' Day

Down over Short Hill Mountain comes the chill
that settles on this white-washed country church,
a quiet freshness, chased by rain, until
the bells call to us from their steeple perch.
The pathway in is gashed with glistening leaves,
bright brilliant scars of autumn's waning days.
Our newly widowed friend Marie still grieves,
her dark eyes veiled to cover sorrow's blaze.
We all glide in, then settle like the frost
that edges the rough grasses in the field.
Our broken prayers for all the ones we've lost
are bound like sheaves, the brittle harvest's yield.
Small crimson berries on the bush outside
lash on the window in a sudden wind,
staccato accompaniment, or nature's chide
to rouse ourselves, and look around, chagrined.
The empty spaces in these pews might be
still laden with the souls who came before,
the jostling cluster of the dead who see
ahead the faint outline of heaven's door.
What winding liturgy of life will lead
us out, what beckoning abundance draw
us in? The mists that linger like our need
hang heavy over fields of fresh cut straw.

Carla Galdo serves *Well-Read Mom* as an editor, writer, and content creator. She has written for a variety of publications including *Humanum: Issues in Family, Culture, and Science and Columbia Magazine.* Carla earned a Masters of Theological Studies from the Pontifical John Paul II Institute for Marriage and Family, and is currently pursuing a Master of Fine Arts in Creative Writing at the University of St. Thomas — Houston. She and her husband homeschool their six children on a small hobby farm in rural Virginia.

LESLEY-ANNE EVANS

Mother, God

I am alone in St. Peter's hush.
Tour groups circle like pods of killer whales
hungry for experience. Three nuns
float by in unearthly robes.

I turn and there you are —
icon of high school art history —
iceberg madonna, luminous in a niche
of shadows. I can't move my feet.

Who can know the keel of pain
that looms within your form,
crushed heart. I'm only twenty five
and not yet a mom. Why am I crying?

When Michelangelo released you
from the stone, your knees and hands
were larger than life. Maybe that's how
you bear this load? With one hand

you hold the lifeless body of your son,
while the other is open to sky,
or fate, or whatever you trust. If only
I were holy like you, Pieta, I could hold

my dying certainty. I could maintain
the Artist's plan is good. Not yet. Doctrine
is a chunk of ice drifting in a cold sea —
too slight to calve; too dense to melt.

Previously published in *The Ekphrastic Review*, January 2023 (digital).

Irish-Canadian **Lesley-Anne Evans** is author of *Mute Swan*, her debut poetry collection from *The St. Thomas Poetry Series* (Toronto, 2021). Her work appears in *The Antigonish Review, Barren, Cascadia Review, CV-2, Ekstasis, Letters* (Yale), and *Quills*, among other periodical publications. Lesley-Anne hosts Feeny Wood, a woodland retreat for creatives and spiritual seekers.

LEE KIBLINGER

The Vanishing Point

I stood in a dusty gallery
with an aged landscape —

framed with
foreground trees
bent inward
beneath blue,
the horizon's steep
sky enfolded over
burgeoning branches,
in view

distant figures,
a lifeless horse,
blurred —
the artist's lines
swallowing,
their end,
a destiny,
inferred

and I wondered —
at its two dimensions,
man-mixed colors,
the curtain of trees
of knowledge,
of life,
framing the scene,
forging skyline —

that what is formed
with words, and dust

could converge
with what's imagined,
a promised line
between earth
and heaven —

so that my eyes
have nowhere else
to go —
but to that point,
invisible, but known,
the place where
storied trees
are fully grown.

Lee Kiblinger is a teacher and late-blooming poet from Tyler, Texas, where she spends her time devouring novels, grading essays, laughing with three teenagers, and enjoying poetry with other Rabbit Room poets. Her work can be found in *Calla Press*, *Kosmeo Magazine*, *Ekstasis Magazine*, and *Heart of Flesh*.

Tamara Nicholl-Smith

Petition
(for Larry Lines 1970-2022)

These are the days
       when phone calls
from friends
       are increasingly likely
       to inform
of some new cancer,
       remission, recurrence.
These are the days
I spend on my knees
       at the front of the church
       in petition to Mary
           clothed in stained light
       sliding folded dollars
       into the brass mouth
of the offering box,
using the slender wood
       to carry flame from one candle to another
before putting it out
       in a dish of sand.

I can see
the light's lineage
       how the candle may hold the flame
but cannot control
       when it is lit
and when it goes out
       by sudden wind — the side chapel door
swinging open in spring
       or the slow spending
       of paraffin wax.

It might appear
I am quite alone,
but the air around the altar
is saturated
        with spent wax, burnt wood,
and a haze of incense —
                where prayers hang —
        like droplets
caught in low clouds
and saints are drawn —
        like deer to graze
in the leafy rain.

Song for the Slow Road

I forget sometimes that I have aged,
that time has turned me snowcapped,
especially when I see you, daughter.
It can be like looking at my own face.

My heart longs with yours,
as you gaze upon the road below,
on fire with red-leafed flame,
your possible future,
riding towards or going past.

When I go to rise, my bones creak
like door hinges craving oil.
Memory twines its vine branches
round the rough porch pillars.
Just yesterday, you were small,
swaddled and scented with milk-breath.

I am not yet ready to yield
to the forgetful mist
though I slow to a lumber
long' the moss-lined lane
caught in the linger of lowing
cows, their plainchant resting
like fog on the far field.

The air cools,
yet I am filled
with a brightness
that defies
the shortening light.

Tamara Nicholl-Smith is a Texas-based poet and workshop leader. Her poetry has appeared on two Albuquerque city bus panels, one parking meter, various radio shows, a spoken-word classical piano fusion album, and in publications, such as *America*, *Ekstasis*, *The Examined Life Journal*, *Kyoto Journal*, and *Joi De Vivre*. She is an MFA candidate in Creative Writing at the University of Saint Thomas (Houston). Her poem on Saint Jerome will be a permanent part of the display featuring a perfect replica of the Peplin Edition of the Gutenberg Bible to be installed at the University of Saint Thomas Library in Houston. She enjoys puns and likes her bourbon neat. Visit her at tamaranichollsmith.com or connect on Twitter @ tnichollsmith.

BETHANY F. BRENGAN

Soul & Body

The way a parent carries
a child after a long day — less
tenderness than twitching patience —
so my soul carries my body.
My soul has taken
my body to the library,
to the park, to see the fireworks blossoming
across the dark; although the whole time
my body tugged on Soul's sleeve:
I have to pee. My feet hurt. I'm
so thirsty I'm gonna diiie.
My soul shells out mornings
to raising Body
out of bed, feeding, cleaning;
evenings out of pocket
to the same work, in reverse.
Soul has no time
of its own. Sometimes, Soul dreams
of the day Body will move
into its own small apartment. But mostly,
Soul focuses on folding
Body's moth-thin limbs
under the bedspread each night —
swallowing panic at the tiny feathers
coating Soul's fingers like flour.

Beatitudes of Disability

"Any person who is diseased, maimed, mutilated, or in any way deformed, so as to be an unsightly or disgusting object, or an improper person to be allowed in or on the streets, highways, thoroughfares, or public places in the city, shall not therein or thereon expose himself or herself to public view, under the penalty of a fine of one dollar for each offense." —City of Chicago ordinance, 1881

Blessed are the tired
for they shall gain patience.
Blessed are the slow and exhausted
for they will notice when another
sparrow falls. Blessed are the pained
for they shall be gentle. Blessed are the lost-
marblers, the mutterers on public
transport, the gimps, the crips, the crazies,
the obsoletes, the invalids, the curiosities,
the ugly, the frightening to nice women
and small children, the unrespectable,
and the unfortunate, for they shall not
be denied. Blessed are you
when you are an uncomfortable reminder
of life's wild, uncategorized growth. Blessed
are you when you are discounted,
anomalized, and filed away. Rejoice,
for God, too, has a body
strangers try not to
stare at in grocery stores.

Bethany F. Brengan is a freelance writer and editor with a contradictory love of both cats and birds. She grew up in Kentucky and now lives in the PNW. She writes about books, comics, disability, and writing. She also writes a lot of poetry. Her work has appeared in *Ninth Letter, Seaside Gothic, Contrary Magazine*, and *Dick Grayson, Boy Wonder: Scholars and Creators on 75 Years of Robin, Nightwing, and Batman*. She can be found at https://medium.com/@bethanybrengan.

WILLIAM STARK

Genesis

Burn.

Be.

Spark, and illuminate —

Flare, like the infinitesimal piercing of
Light that first breaks like a wave on the
Edge of the flame-roaring dawn. And the
Word, singularity, sings in that burgeoning,
Flashing explosion of fiery verse that is
Music far-off beyond world-ancient stars — while all
Growth and unfurling now floods from that origin,
Blazing and blooming, begotten from nothingness,
Spoken, awakened, and rampant in radiance:
Infinite poetry rippling with fruitfulness,
Surging creation in billows of depthless span —

And pulsing still in everyday,
Though ages distant from that sound:
A yearning music on the wind,
Scents of strange flowers we have not found,
With subtle longing harmony,
All echo, shimmer, tantalize;
The ripples of infinity
Yet hum and hymn through sea and skies.

Listen — the threads of the world still all thrum that chord:
Birth of all things, in which all things will be restored —

For glory waits and strains, a rising storm:
A gathering grace's fury found in love.

Our air is tense with thunder, taut, and warm:
We wait the Word poured out like rain above.

Creation aches to snap its stretching seams
And loose a splendor now unseen, unknown;
Our earthbound being quakes with swelling streams
Of Heaven's laughter bursting like the dawn.

Now as this present shadow shreds away
New music floods horizon's curtains furled:
A far green country under rising day,
A bright undying song beyond this world —

As at the first, so evermore shall be
Creation's echoes swell to final harmony:
Fabric of fiery notes, sublime verse of one Word.

Easter, Earthed

Dust you are; to dust you shall return,
For you are earthen: clay and roughened loam,
A mold of craze-cracked bowls and poorer soil,
A human humus, rich only with that rot
Which roots the sod of Eden's fateful tree.

Yet in this season God Himself is thrown
And glazed and fired — fallowed, furrowed deep.
He dons the fractured humane vessel's form —
A harrowed field, wound painfully with thorns,
Torn ground that groans under a cross-like tree —
And shatters, breaks itself, a bowl that spills
A price of blood, like wine on clattered shards.

Still limn these shards with living gold; the bowl
Now bears its breaking-lines, yet gleams as whole
And heals all others. Dying dust with Him
Will flower as a verdant-tended field,
To cup and cultivate that growth of God
In human earth that lifts the tree of life.

Author's Note: In this poem, I draw on the imagery of *kintsugi*, a Japanese technique for repairing broken pottery by filling in the cracks with gold, making the finished product far more beautiful and valuable than the original piece. This image of broken pottery (made from fired clay) resonated for me with the idea of "earthiness," which in turn suggested a variety of additional metaphors involving earth used in fields and agriculture.

William Stark is a student of classics and chemistry at Furman University in Greenville, SC, where he works as the editor-in-chief of the journal *Christo et Doctrinae*. He writes primarily formal poetry inspired by the works of Gerard Manley Hopkins, Malcolm Guite, and Seamus Heaney, and he is published at *Christo et Doctrinae*, the Furman *Echo*, and *Stories of Yearning*. William can be contacted at williamstark2003@gmail.com or www.linkedin.com/in/williamjeffreystark.

KLARA KINMAN

From Dust, To Dust

The dust dances in the window
        of my gramma's living room,

swimming around her
               dead houseplants
and bathing in the wax
        of the yankee candles
               that rest on the windowsill.

I sit with my face pressed
        against the warm glass.
My body communes with the sunlight
        as the dust,
playful,
        brushes against my cheeks.

Once I read that dust is
        pieces of ourselves,

that we shed dust like snakes
        shed exoskeletons.

What else is there to do with all this living?

In a lifetime,
we collect heaps of the stuff,
        soft piles of our old selves
thrown out
        with stained napkins
               and crinkled candy wrappers.

I reach out my hand,

       swirl my fingers in a circular motion,
watch the dust

rise from the windowsill,
       rise from the withered christmas cactus,
           rise from the cinnamon candles,

rise and become alive again,
dancing.

Klara Kinman is a poet and artist from Louisville, Kentucky. She is currently pursuing a B.A. in English from Asbury University. Klara serves as the Associate Editor-In-Chief of Asbury's undergraduate literary magazine, *The Asbury Review*.

CYNTHIA SOWERS

A Marginal Revelation

We were angry.

But even so:
there was time
when Leviathan curved and blew
in all innocence;
young lions at nightfall
came out to hunt
according to law.

We were hurt and torn.

But there was a time
when no poisonous herb grew
and death was not intended;
the land did not mourn
nor did all who dwell
in it languish.

Still — we withdrew
into what resembles exile.

But there was a time
for hearing each particular thing
and each part of each particular thing
and each single part of each single part
in multiplied difference
according to the designated work
of matter tasked to resound
in song its unique,
unparalleled joy.

But now:

afternoon light
slipping between closed blinds
falling blurred, uneven,
disfigured on the rug
under the dining room table
(glimpsed for a second),
scandalously lovely;
abject:

"Will you talk to me?"

Cynthia Sowers was a Senior Lecturer at the Residential College of the University of Michigan, where she developed and taught interdisciplinary courses for the Arts and Ideas in the Humanities Program. Her work is focused on the engagement of literature and the visual arts as immediate practice while entangled in history. Publications include poetry, drawings, and paintings in *Solum Journal*; poetry in *Amethyst Review*; and a short story, "A Trap to Catch the Earth," in *The Carolina Quarterly*.

FICTION

Katy Carl

Pantheon

The white house on the prominent avenue behind the spreading oaks, one of dozens like it throughout the city, shimmered in its floodlights. A shine like this, houses like these, had figured in Rachel's dreams from the onset of memory. To pull up to the columned porch now in graduate-student Peter's car, to hear the oyster shell drive crunching under the wheels: it hollowed out a space under her ribs into which she felt the chilled air rushing.

Oxygen high, hot flush of adrenaline: not weeks ago, but days, she had been a studious nobody in a back corner of a stucco rowhome, hiding one contraband library book at a time in the waistband of an apron or the pocket of a long, dark skirt. Headscarves, stockings, three services on Sabbaths. Now her dandelion-colored hem grazed her at midthigh, where dark hairs prickled her. If she had paid more attention to the lurid headlines in the grocery checkout, she could have planned ahead to solve this problem. But she had been taught to be afraid of those magazines with their tall neon letters; it had been said their influence could control her, possess her. The force of this fear had not yet faded although it no longer drove her. She needed a path out, yes, but she wanted to grade the path herself.

Rachel thrilled to the word *sinner*. It sizzled over her skin. It was what she was. She had stolen money, more than a hundred dollars, from the community's metal cashbox. She had lied about where she was going. She had planned for a time when everyone else would be in the meeting room; she had cooked up a pretext about preparing something in the kitchen for fellowship. On the way to the bus stop, she had laughed and laughed. She was never going back. She might be a sinner, but she was a free sinner. The oyster shell drive crunched under her feet.

A backbeat shook the wooden floorboards of the porch and jarred her heartbeat into corresponding rhythm. Nothing would trap her again, she thought, as she walked under the cut-glass lintel that glinted iridescent in the floodlights, as she and Peter melted into the clamoring crowd.

Later, decades later, working with her students as a university professor, Rachel would use this moment to illustrate how the dazzling aesthetics of a lifestyle can blind naïve people to its dubious ethics. But now, as Peter stepped out of the car and walked around to open her door, now before the invention of the cell phone, now before the common incursion of the Internet, now before she ever held a job or a scholarship or a bank account in her own name, Rachel saw the house with washed eyes. She saw it then as the city of the New Jerusalem, where they shall have no need of lamps or of the sun. And there would be no temple, for the city itself would be their temple.

Peter and Rachel walked up the oyster shell drive and then up four red brick steps between the wide white columns and under a transom of stained glass set in sharp squares and diamonds. As they shouldered through a crowd of swaying fawn-thin girls in shimmering tank tops and dark jeans, the golden glow of the chandelier fell on Peter's wheat-shock of hair.

Rachel decided to make the white house her temple, in the privacy of her mind. No one need know what went on in that privacy: not her stepmother mewling *I just wish my only daughter trusted me more*, not the pastor who was no longer her pastor intoning *A secret kept from me is a secret kept from God and God is not mocked, He will know, He knows even now*. No more. Rachel was free. Free. She could not have known then, she would later have to soothe herself, she could not have known how trapped she still was.

Rachel made up her mind then, too, to marry Peter and to go wherever he could take her, as far away from the life she'd escaped as possible. As though this decision were well known to both of them and yet of no real significance, she smiled up at Peter and then let go of his hand.

Long before her family had enclosed itself behind walls, Rachel remembered seeing houses like this one from the back window of her parents' car. When she was so little that they still lived in the house with the breezeway, so little that they still had not switched churches or moved to the compound, she wondered about life inside these big houses, these shrines to security and prosperity. This was so long ago that the crash had not yet taken her mother, back when they had still owned a car instead of driving the communally-owned vans.

Now she was inside the white house behind the columns, really inside it: she was really herself, she existed, she could verify it. Her feet slid in sandals on the checkerboard tile; her eyes dilated to let in the low light. She could brush her arm against the arm of another person, and the other person would pull back from her and look at her strangely. Apparently you didn't do that, she noted: that was one of the things you really weren't supposed to do. It could sometimes be hard to tell which those were.

Losing track of Peter for a moment, she pressed through the crowded grand hall, where a dance floor had been set up in front of the unlit fireplace. A tall, long-limbed pair of dancers, costumed in Mardi Gras attire—a white man in black, a black woman in white, sequins on their sleeves, flowers in her curls—leaned heavily on each other and oscillated in no visible relationship to the tempo of the music.

Across the chessboard floor, past the debutantes' staircase, under the long gallery, along the wide back corridor lined with old church pews that had been pried out of some chapel and newly lined with red velour cushions, Rachel passed into the huge kitchen as nonchalantly as if she had been at coffee hour after a sermon.

The massive kitchen had been modernized with gleaming tile and with panels of pine weathered to mimic driftwood. A yawning hearth of limewashed brick swallowed one wall. A yawning fraternity pledge sprawled along the baseboard of the other.

Five or six wearers of glasses sat, drinking hard and listening harder, in a breakfast nook to one side. In the corner seat, an animated young man with vertical black curls held forth on the history of streetcars. Their table was empty of everything but their cups, and that was funny. Until now Rachel had thought parties revolved around food: black plastic catering platters, maybe, like those she saw in the cold case at the grocery store; or, in keeping with the fairytale feeling the house gave her, crystal serving dishes like those that might be found in the kinds of books she had been secretly reading. Instead, across the ice-white granite countertops, there lay greasy cardboard flats printed all over with garish red and blue patterns.

A punchbowl without a ladle hunched in a corner of the granite counter. A red plastic cup had been dropped in it for use as a scoop, floating among chunks of fruit. Rachel, accustomed to serving, filled two more red cups full to their brims and made her way back through the crowd to where Peter had started some conversation with another male student. The other student seemed to be boring him; when she walked up, he turned to her with a mild but definitely pleased look.

"Hey, I'd almost given up on you," he said.

Peter smiled and raised an eyebrow as he took a full cup from her, feeling its heft.

"Go easy there," he said.

"I do this all the time," she lied.

He mimicked her shrug. "Okay then," he said, "you know best."

She knew that she knew nothing. Did Peter also realize this? The strap of the messenger bag cut into her shoulder where it met her neck.

"Why don't you put that down?" he said.

Her money itched her skin, a crumpled flap inside her bra. Her awkward bag contained only a library book, the long dark skirt, some scratchy nylons, and the headscarf.

"Where can I leave it?"

"There's a bunch of stuff in the front closet. I think some people are planning to stay the night. You could just throw it there."

Obediently she ran off, her steps paced to the beat of the thumping music, to throw the bag into the closet. She instantly felt much better. When she returned, Peter smiled and placed his hand on the place where she had sewn into the dress an oval cutout to show the curve of her back. Her skin fizzed with the contrary sensations of chilled air and warm contact on unaccustomed exposures.

In the huge main room, fans whirled under the balustrade. Dancing women frisked and wove in sporadic patterns to the thump of the music. Rachel felt as visible as an onion in a bin of apples, and as appealing. She thought of Kitty at the ball in her pink froth of tulle, Anna in black velvet.

Her own yellow minidress with its lumpy seams made her feel like a beacon was trained on her. She thought now with sheepishness of the delight she had felt in finding the pattern and the fabric at the bottom of an old cardboard box in the dormitory closet, the thrill of fear while piecing the dress together— she had claimed to be making placemats, and no one had questioned her. Continually under suspicion for every reason and no reason, she had learned to lie early and often, to lie fluently and well. When she later said she had made a mistake with the placemats, that they had turned out so badly she'd thrown them away, she had been punished for wasting community resources, but no one had even suspected her of not telling the truth.

The fabric, a yellow wool and polyester blend, fuzzed thickly around her body. She could feel a heat rash beginning on her thighs. The wild thought skipped across her mind that she should tear the dress off and run through the room and out the door in the black track shorts and sports bra she had stolen yesterday to wear underneath.

The cold, sweating punch cup in her hand blocked this thought effectively. There was no place she could put it down; she had to keep holding it. Its slick weight anchored her.

All this time they moved through the party; Peter shouted greetings and gestured at people with his drinking hand, while with his other hand he kept hold of Rachel's back. They moved across the chessboard floor and out through French doors into a courtyard behind the house. Around them a low box hedge marked out a wide quadrangle. In the center of the square a copper fountain, long since gone teal with verdigris, bubbled quietly into a ring of red bricks. In one corner, under a dim overhang of Spanish moss, a wrought-iron bench, painted white, listed to one side. The bench looked in the low light like its own ghost.

He led her to the bench, and they sat down unevenly. The hand he had placed on her back made its way to the outside of her hip. His arm tightened around her. Her muscles hummed with delight and terror, not sure how to refuse this contact or to ask for more, not sure even what she ought to do, wanted to do, ought to want.

"You'd better tell me what's really going on," Peter said. "You're not from any magazine staff. Why did you lie?"

Three days ago, Rachel and Peter had met at what she would later learn was a famous coffee house in the French Quarter, under dozens of lazily spiraling ceiling fans. The coffee house had been her first venture outside of her community's stucco house in the past eight years, except to visit the library, corner grocery, Walmart, and the abandoned warehouse that had served as her father's church. The warehouse was part of the same compound as the stucco house, where several of the core families lived. When she left, Rachel had felt at first like a groundhog emerging from hibernation. The corners of her vision had been blurry, as if she were filming her own experience through a soft-focus lens.

That day, like tonight, Rachel had been nerved by the boldness of terror. She had coolly lied to everyone she saw. The people she met first—a gentle, old, wealthy, vacationing couple walking slowly together in matched khaki shorts and Margaritaville T-shirts, tube socks and cushioned Reeboks—had sized her up far more quickly than she was able to do the same to them. To them (though she would only understand this later) her outfit had signaled a Hasidic girl on holiday from the East Coast, separated from her family and trying to find them before she or they caved into panic.

Not fully aware of the context in which they were placing her, but happy to exploit their obvious confusion, Rachel had played along with what she could follow from their misunderstanding. She had pretended that her putative parents had told her to meet them at the coffee house, you know, the coffee house? . . . that one place . . .? The couple had instantly sparked to the name Café du Monde.

This was when Rachel still did many things that no one did. Up to this point her notions of what you could and could not do had been absolute, totalized. She had lived inside the continually shrinking perimeter of *Thou shalt*. Outside its borders lay the margin of *Thou shalt not*, which encompassed things she now knew others did every day, every hour. Once she stepped over that line, it seemed to her that nothing was out of bounds anymore, that she could do anything at all.

So after thanking the vacationers profusely and running off in the sweltering white afternoon, it was a short step for Rachel to march up to the best-looking young man in the place and, heart hammering, ask him where the party was. (In the one glossy magazine Rachel had dared to steal a look at in Walmart, when she was supposed to be shopping for cleaning supplies, she had run across a short story in which people were always asking each other where "the party" was, as though there could only be one party taking place at a time, or only one worth attending.)

He had told her where he was headed that weekend. Then Rachel, facing Peter across the wobbly table, had cobbled together another tarradiddle. This time, she claimed she was a reporter doing a profile on the family that owned the white house where the party was. Yes, the Bonsecour family: could he please get her in; could he introduce her?

In the shade of the open pavilion, Peter had looked at Rachel strangely, but then he nodded, once, with a half-knowing smile on his face. Now on the painted bench, as Rachel's face creased like an infant's, he patted her back awkwardly.

"Oh God, so sorry. I didn't want to upset you, I'm just curious. I would have brought you here tonight anyway. And I might as well come clean, too. I don't know the Bonsecours. They own this house, but they don't live here."

Rachel sniffed, cleared her throat. "They don't?"

"No, they rent it out. My friend Wade's parents rent it."

Even the bifurcated meanings of the word "rent" were enough to slow Rachel down then: she needed a moment to figure out who was doing the renting if they both were renting. No one had ever talked to her, or in front of her, in any significant way about any kind of business or money matter. It wasn't supposed to matter to her, she had been unequivocally told. She was supposed to marry, and her husband was supposed to take care of all of that. And though she did not want this kind of marriage, she could see the appeal of it: you could flourish in obscurity, while you let someone else worry about the messy business of survival.

"They're out of town," Peter went on, surmising from Rachel's silence that she didn't understand.

So then, were the partygoers all *trespassing*? Anxiety locked her muscles. There flashed in her mind the image of herself in handcuffs and then in the kind of jail cell she had seen in a cartoon as a young child, before all television had been forbidden her. She had been sequestered away, her head filled with invented terrors to try to prevent her from knowing. Now she began to understand, sitting in the garden next to Peter, that the greater danger could dwell in what you did not know.

But Peter read her pause in his own way. "It's fine. He said I could bring whoever. Don't worry. Really, you're okay? I didn't mean to upset you. It's much better if you aren't writing something. That way we can just have fun."

"Okay." The syllables fell out of her mouth in a whisper. She made an effort to smile.

Peter raised his arm now and draped it around her bare shoulders. His casual slowness suggested that he, too, did this all the time. But then she had been lying; perhaps he was lying now, too, only with his body. Rachel sat in the grip of a physical emotion she couldn't name. It paralyzed her even as it filled her with a wish to move, how and toward what she didn't know. She shivered. She had no words to give to what was happening to her. Those words she acquired later, too late.

Peter didn't notice her distress. He told her all about his research: about ancient Greek and Roman modes and rituals of religious devotion, about the mysteries, the initiations. He told her about the Roman Pantheon, still in use as a Catholic basilica, and then, on a tangent, about the entertainment house by the same name, in London, in the eighteenth century.

Unable to respond, Rachel shaped her mouth to the lip of the cup and drank the purple liquid. It tasted both sweet and astringent. She gulped it down so fast that Peter laughed at her.

"Really, slow down," he said, "unless you need to be good and drunk. Do you?"

Rachel laughed.

"I've tried it with Triple Sec," he went on, "and with Grand Marnier, but never with spiced rum like that." At the distance of memory, Rachel could process this as mere conversation-making, but in the moment, she combed the statement for meaning, like prophecy. "Have you? How do you make it?" he asked.

"Make what?"

"Sangria," Peter said, and that was how Rachel learned that word. With a smirk he added: "You really don't do this all the time, do you?"

Rachel hid the shape her mouth was making by finishing her drink. When it was done, she could smile up at him. Then the thumping from within the house suddenly ended. From the open doors across the courtyard, they heard yelling and groans. Someone had put on a recording of classical harpsichord minuets. There came an even louder cacophony, a wall of complaint, which ended only with the music.

"Okay, okay, but what about this?" shouted a male voice. A whir and a click were followed by the swells of trumpets, saxophones. More grumbling followed, but this time they were grumbles of acquiescence: this was New Orleans. People couldn't exactly get away with naysaying jazz.

Peter's face lit up. "Don't you want to dance?" he asked. He took Rachel by the hand and pulled her up from the seat. She stumbled; while they were sitting on the bench her right leg had fallen asleep. Now it began with dozens of hot stabs to come awake again. With every other step she had to hitch to shift her weight partly off of it.

Peter took her hand again and swung her, first into an underarm spin and then into a loping, round cotillion step she struggled to follow. She lurched right as he went left, left as he went right. Her knee collided with his. The toe of his oxford wedged under her instep in its sandal. Her still-tingling leg buckled. She hit the chessboard floor bottom first. A roar of laughter flew up from all around. The sound echoed off the ceiling like sheets of rain being flung down in a thunderstorm. She tried to get up, but the knee of her sleeping leg gave way. The wall of hilarity flattened her.

Someone flicked the chandelier lights on and off as if they were browning out. When the flicking ended, the lights remained off. Peter and Rachel could only see by the dim glow from the upstairs wall sconces along the gallery upstairs.

She saw knees, cleanly shaped, below rumpled khaki shorts, on the dusty checkerboard tiles. Rachel looked away from the tiles and back at the knees, which had not moved.

"You didn't hit your head, did you?" said the owner of the knees, clearly Peter, who else? The question mattered, but Rachel could only hear it as if through a closed door. Its answer might explain the fog in her vision and the ache in her skull. Then again, the thought of an ambulance horrified her: explanations, next of kin, discovery, return to the compound where the elders would claim their rights over her. She shook her head no.

"Good," he said. There was no one looking at them after all. He held out a hand to help her rise. "Let's go upstairs."

Along the upper railing of the hallway and up and down the staircase there sat partygoers lolling with more cold red cups, more greasy cardboard boxes, more of whatever they were smoking that made that pungent smell. They climbed past them up the arching debutante staircase. Each step creaked lightly underfoot as the soft wood curved beneath its carpet to support them. The red velour, once grand but now stained and greyed with age in the center of the tread, caused the soles of her sandals to slip around. They were the only shoes she owned—a pair of old knockoff Birkenstocks whose treads were severely ablated.

She was sweating and trembling by the time they reached the landing, not from exertion but because, having already slipped once, she was afraid of doing so again. The next fall felt inevitable and, Rachel feared, could ruin everything. But what *was* everything? The fog in her head annoyed her.

At the top of the staircase, Peter reached for her hand. This marked the boundary line of physical contact beyond which the elders of the enclave had warned her not to go. To prove she did not agree with them, she tucked herself beneath Peter's arm and pressed her side against his as they walked. She could not help but be aware of the pressure of her hip against his thigh, of the absurd difference in their heights and the texture of their skin, the firmness of the muscle in his, the softness in hers. Even his body temperature seemed a degree or two warmer.

She had been given no language but that of sin for the situation in which she found herself, and so she figured that anything she did from now on was either stained irreparably or only redeemable retroactively, but either way necessary to live through to the end now that she had begun. She might as well, she reasoned, do what she wanted. But what did she want? She had no language for this either. Her mind fell back on Anna and Vronsky: kisses followed in brisk succession by an infant. Well, and wasn't this a reasonable thing to want? Rachel asked herself. Where on earth else, she asked, did she think she was going from here tonight?

They had walked all along the gallery and then down a smaller, darker hallway where most of the doors were closed. A scattering of couples sat along the walls of this hallway, separated from the rest of the party, some on benches or seats, some on the floor, some on long window seats that stretched between high brocade drapes. The light from the high windows fell on the couples' bodies in long blue shapes.

Peter stepped up to a double door and knocked softly on one side of it.

"Just left, man. No one in there now," said a voice from the floor.

Slowly Peter swung the door inward. The hinge skirled as he replied to the voice, "Thanks, man." He pulled Rachel by her hand, unresisting, into the room after him.

It was a high-ceilinged bedroom, filled with old, dark wooden furniture, lit only with the dusky scraps of half-shadow thrown from the floodlights in front of the house and filtered through leaves. A smell like stale bread filled the air. Without dropping Rachel's hand Peter leaned over the tall bed, checked over the sheets as though looking for something he'd lost there, and shook his head. He chose a pillow that had been propped against the headboard and set it against the wall. He sat down on the floor with his back against the pillow and patted the carpet next to him. Rachel, uncertainly, sat down beside him, adjusting her hemline.

"Oh, don't worry about that," Peter said. With a smile he slid his index finger along her outer thigh until it stuck under the hem. He pushed the skirt back to where it had been before, only an inch or so, but Rachel frowned.

Peter's smile, too, faded.

He hitched himself a little closer to her. He kissed her neck where the messenger bag strap had marked it. He kissed her jawline, her cheekbone, her temple. He put his hand on her knee but yanked it away at the feel of

66

the hair, with a little laugh that wasn't funny. He covered her lips with his so long that finally, she had to break away with a gasp.

Peter murmured something under his breath. She couldn't understand him at first. Then he showed her how to take little breaths, and when. "Like swimming."

She had never been swimming. She could not find words to tell him this. She began to laugh uncontrollably, to shake with laughter.

"Shh, shh," he said, putting a hand gently to her mouth. "We have to be quiet. Look, I'll lock it."

He turned away from her and crawled over to the door and reached up to the handle, a lever with a thumb-lock that he secured with a click. Then he scooted back and, making a swipe at playfulness, grabbed her in a hug that knocked her down. She began to cry out and he covered her mouth again. "Shh, shh," he repeated.

They went on like this for what felt, to Rachel, like a long time. When she remembered it later, when she was ready to remember it, she realized it must not have been more than five or ten minutes. The paralysis had returned; it seemed to live now in her hipbones and to be anchoring her to the carpet. When Peter pinned her down she couldn't move, couldn't speak. She felt as immobilized as if she were under an anesthetic. The fabric of his cargo shorts chafed against the wool of her dress, roughened against her thigh. He pressed down so hard it hurt her. She began to try to tell him this, but he had grown strangely distant now, as if listening to music only he could hear.

"Shh, shh," he repeated. "Don't worry, it's okay."

He reached for the waistband of her shorts, and she shook her head frantically. He paused.

"No, you're right," he said. "Can't have you getting pregnant." He removed his hand from her clothing, seemed to adjust his own instead. She felt heat on the skin over her ribs, across her dress, but—even she knew that this was not how this worked.

"There. That should be okay." He began to move again.

It wasn't okay. It wasn't. Her ribs hurt. This was not how it worked. Was he having a seizure? Should she say something? He was sweating. He seemed as though he might be about to begin crying until he grunted, slipped, and lay still with his face down in the pillow. She sat up and looked at him.

"Are you all right?" she asked. He didn't respond at first. She sat for a moment worrying about ambulances again, feeling vaguely at fault for whatever had gone wrong here.

At length, Peter nodded without lifting his head.

"Fine, thanks." He spoke half into the pillow. He seemed to be falling asleep.

She held very still and examined the loops and ripples of the ceiling medallion. A broad-armed ceiling fan had been wired through the medallion's apex. Then she stood up, feeling lightheaded. At some point she had stepped out of her sandals. She picked them up off the floor by their straps and walked out. Not until later would she remember her messenger bag; she would never go back for it. Not until later would she notice her bruises. Not until later would she know what to call this.

She walked back down the hall, downstairs, across the chessboard floor, the thumping porch, the bricks of the esplanade in front of the house. The beat grew fainter as she stepped on the damp green grass of the lawn, which was now being irrigated by sprinklers and glistening slickly in the glare from the floodlights. Battalions of blade-like shadows rose up on the path in front of her, cast by the leaves of hostas and hydrangeas. She ignored the bricks' grit against the soles of her feet until they registered a sliding sensation, followed by a piercing one: she looked down to see her own foot outlined against green-edged rectangular prisms of glass, sprayed from a car's broken windshield. Only then did she remember that she was still carrying her sandals in her hands.

She sat on the grass, brushed her soles off, put her sandals back on, and walked down the sidewalk until she came to a bus stop shelter. Here she sat down to wait, not entirely knowing where she intended to go other than as far away as she could get from the white house, from its glamour, its pallid façade.

Katy Carl is editor in chief of *Dappled Things* magazine and author of *As Earth Without Water*, a novel (Wiseblood Books, 2021), and *Fragile Objects*, short stories (2023). Her fiction and essays have appeared in *Fare Forward, Windhover, Vita Poetica, Belle Ombre, Across the Margin, Exposition Review, Psaltery & Lyre, Sostenuto, Mom Egg Review, Genealogies of Modernity, St. Louis* magazine, *Mere Orthodoxy, Church Life Journal*, and the *Mid/South Anthology,* among others. She is also a senior affiliate fellow of the Program for Research on Religion and Urban Civil Society located at the University of Pennsylvania, and she holds an MFA in fiction from the University of St. Thomas — Houston. She lives in the Houston area with her husband and family.

John Cormier

Cricket

The fluorescent lights in the waiting room drone overhead like a swarm of angry insects. I've been here for six hours now, outside the emergency room at Summit Medical Center with my sister, waiting for some kind of update. This was becoming a yearly tradition, the two of us sitting here while Mom gets her stomach pumped. I don't know what she took this time, only that it was clearly too much, and Katie found her face down on the kitchen floor in the throes of a seizure, gasping for air like a fish out of water. Katie was apparently too shaken to get in the ambulance with her so she called me to come pick her up. Nearly two hours ago she balled up her sweatshirt like a pillow and stretched out across a bench to try and get some sleep, leaving me to keep my vigil alone. I don't care that it's four in the morning, I'm just disgusted that they've managed to drag me back into their circus.

I look over at my little sister and realize I've been chewing a hole in the inside of my cheek. We haven't been in the same room in over six months and I recognize her less now than I could then. She's lost even more weight and it looks like she hasn't washed her hair in over a week. I can see the vertebrae poking up through her tank top like someone stretched cheap green fabric over a mountain range. I shudder at the realization that at twenty-six Katie looks just like Mom did when I was ten. The thought makes me look away.

I stand to unzip my jacket, then lay it across her and walk out the front door of the waiting room into the crisp predawn air of Tennessee in August with the urge to run to my car and drive away itching in the back of my head. Instead I fish a pack of cigarettes from my pocket and light next to a "NO SMOKING" sign. Absentmindedly it occurs to me that it sounds like angry insects out here, too. An orchestra of crickets play their music in the grass. I close my eyes and listen.

The first time I noticed something was wrong with Mom, I was eleven years old. She pulled me out of school in the middle of the day. Katie was only eight at the time and she was already sitting in the backseat when I climbed in next to her. Mom looked back at us, her eyes wide and wild with pupils like pinpricks, and said, "I thought we could all go see a movie together! How does that sound?"

Katie and I cheered and laughed and it felt like we were getting away with something. She drove us to a cheap cineplex on the edge of town and sat us in the back row of a stuffy little theater playing some cheesy movie about an animated cat. Ten minutes in she shook three pills out of an orange plastic bottle and swallowed them down with a drink from my Pepsi. By the end of the movie, I couldn't wake her up. When the usher saw us he was too embarrassed to do anything. Once he was sure she was still breathing, he left us alone and only came by once with a bucket of popcorn for Katie and me. We didn't touch the popcorn but I held Katie's hand and we watched that movie three more times before Mom woke up.

"Evan?"

The sound of Katie's voice pulls me back to the present. Her purple sunken eyes are caked with last night's mascara and she's wearing my jacket which swallows up her fragile frame.

I flick away the rest of my cigarette as she walks over to me. I say, "So, is she out of it yet? Have the doctors said anything?"

She shakes her head, still not fully awake. "No, I just wasn't sure where you went. The woman at the desk said she saw you come out here." She bites her lip, then looks away and says, "I thought you might have left."

I just nod and look at my watch. This is the longest we've waited on a night like this, and I am starting to wonder what the holdup might be. I pull two more cigarettes from my pack, then pass one to Katie after lighting them.

She sends a plume of smoke up to the sky and stares out ahead at one of the last visible stars hanging over the horizon. "Evan?"

"Yeah?"

Katie keeps her eyes locked on that far-off star. "She's gonna make it, right?"

"Are you kidding?" I lean away from her a little bit. The thought hadn't even occurred to me. "This is Mom we're talking about. She's like a Weeble, remember? 'Weebles wobble but they don't fall down'?" There's a trace of humor in my voice, but it quickly leaves me and exhaustion replaces it. "Besides, there's not a drug on this planet that could kill that woman." I punctuate this fact by flicking ash from the tip of my cigarette.

She nods once, then wraps her arms around her stomach. It isn't

71

cold, but I catch her shivering every so often.

I remember when seeing her like this would have broken me. When we were kids she always looked at me like I was her knight, and I would do anything I could to shield her from Mom's endless string of self-destructive tendencies. Some nights when Mom was too broke to get loaded, she would run screaming through the house about how Katie and I were the reason she was poor and couldn't keep a man around. I would take Katie and lock us in my room, then turn the radio up so loud we couldn't hear her anymore. If I was able to convince Katie to start dancing, she would forget all about Mom and we would laugh and flail around to bad pop songs until it was safe to come out. When Katie was fifteen, I caught her trying on Mom's clothes and styling her hair like Mom's in the mirror. I completely lost my shit and yelled at her for half an hour. Katie wouldn't look at me the same after that. She drifted away from me and closer to Mom, and I pulled away from them both.

She breaks me from my reverie again: "Do you remember the trip to Disneyland?"

The question catches me off-guard. She's looking at me now and there's something desperate and urgent in her eyes, something important. I let go of an exasperated sigh as the memory returns to me. It was two years after the incident at the cineplex.

I say, "Yeah, I remember. She woke us up in the middle of the night and told us we were going to Disneyland."

We made it as far as the Texas panhandle and stayed with our Uncle Eddie for three weeks. The truth was, we were running away. Mom had moved her dealer in with us and he acted like he owned us. Mom was always covered in bruises, but wouldn't leave him no matter now much we begged her to.

Katie looks away from me and tightens her lips. For the first time in year she looks sure of something. "Do you know why she finally got us out of there?"

I bunch up my eyebrows and tilt my head to the side. "What do you mean? She got fed up. She was sick of the abuse."

"That man got her pregnant." The words come out of her quietly. "When he found out, he kicked it out of her." Katie drops the last of her cigarette and grinds the life out of it beneath her toe. "You always tried to protect me from that sort of thing, so I thought you knew."

She's rambling now, her eyes feral and manic. She continues, "She told me when I was eighteen. I thought I was pregnant." Her hands fold over just below her navel. "When I told her, she told me that story. I don't know why, she just told me."

I'm thankful that the wall is there to catch me. "Jesus Christ, Katie!" The words explode out of me and I bury my face in my hands. "Why the fuck are you telling me this now?"

A wave of revulsion rolls through me as I try to imagine what life would have been like with another child around for Mom to neglect. A warped vision of a younger Katie runs through my head, and I take deep breaths to fight back the creeping panic. For a moment I'm thankful that I didn't have to live through that.

The resolve in Katie's eyes dwindles and her hands drop to her sides. She stands silently for a moment looking every bit like a lost little girl and sidesteps my question with one of her own: "If Mom makes it . . . will you please move back home?"

I can't bring myself to look her in the eyes so I stare at the ground. "We're not having this conversation, not again. I can't go back there. I can't live in that house, and you shouldn't either." My mouth tastes like bile as I finally face her. She looks like freshly blown glass, all rigid and crystalline, ready to shatter. Something about seeing her like this unties the knot in my stomach and I sigh. "Look . . . my place is cramped, but if I moved some stuff around I could put you up for a while. Just long enough to get you out of that hell hole."

Two years ago, I made my escape. I saved up enough money working third-shift jobs in the industrial park outside of Lebanon to rent a rundown apartment in Nashville. It was a shit hole, but it was mine. Every couple of months, Katie would call, begging me to "come home," as if that place was ever a home to either of us. Last year I got sick of hearing it and told her that if it was so bad there, then she should just leave. She broke down sobbing and said something about how Mom would die without both of us. I made the comment that us being there our whole lives hadn't done much to slow her down; then the line went dead. Katie hated when I talked about Mom like that—when I told the truth.

Now the look in her eyes is conflicted, as if the prospect of freedom is finally tempting enough. Katie has been in recovery twice, but so far it hasn't helped. She's been using Mom as a yard stick for years, trying to see how close she can get to the edge and not fall over. Mom had been using

Katie, too. Enabling Katie's addictions meant that she never had to party alone if she didn't want to.

I say, "Look, I'm not saying it'll be easy, and there are a lot of ground rules we'll have to set, but . . . just say the word and we'll get it done." I feel like a worm, knowing how much this will devastate Mom, but I gave up on her a long time ago, and an outdated version of myself is begging me not to give up on Katie.

The morning sun's first rays crest the horizon as we stare at each other, our eyes both tired and conflicted, when a haggard woman in blue scrubs steps out of the hospital waiting room.

"Are you Mrs. Gibson's children?" she asks.

I am twenty-nine years old and I am so sick of that question. Katie loops her arms around one of mine, squeezes it tightly, and says, "Yes, Katherine is our mother. Can you please tell us what's going on?"

The woman runs a hand through her thick, disheveled hair and says, "I'm going to need you two to come inside."

Katie and I sit side-by-side for twenty minutes as the doctor walks us through the last hour of Mom's life. Ultimately, she suffered a massive coronary, and they were unable to stabilize her heart rhythm. It stopped beating while I was trying to convince my sister to abandon her.

The doctor says we can go see her if we want. Katie takes my hand and tries to pull me along, but I don't budge. I tell her to go, that I just need a minute. That I'll be fine. Mercifully, she leaves and I cry. Not because I miss my mother. Not because I was never going to hear her voice again. I cry from the shame that the first thing that hit me when I heard she was dead was relief. The sobs rack my body and a pain forms behind my eyes that feels both unbearable and deserved. I cry until my lungs burn. I cry until my ribs ache and I think I might hyperventilate. I cry until a memory hits me and I double over with my hands in my hair as I relive the last time I cried this hard.

I was five years old. Mom took me to the park, and while I played, I caught a cricket. We had recently watched Pinocchio together, so I decided to call the cricket Jiminy and ran through the park with him in my hands. I lost my balance, fell, and crushed the cricket in my fist. When Mom found me, my cries were silent, but they shook all through my body. She knelt down in front of me, smoothed my hair, and said, "Baby, what are you crying for? Don't you know if you bury him and wish hard enough, the Blue Fairy will make him real again?" It was exactly the kind of lie to tell a child. We dug a small hole when I finally stopped crying, and covered him with dirt. After I made my wish and opened my eyes, Mom pointed at the grass where a cricket was hopping away.

I catch my breath and decide that it's best to go ahead and get this over with now. When I stand to go find Katie, I notice her sweatshirt still rolled up in a ball on the bench where she was sleeping earlier. I snatch it up, causing a hunk of white plastic to fall out of the pocket on the side. Tentatively, I reach down and pick up the pregnancy test. I stare down at the tiny blue plus sign as the buzz of angry insects hum in the light fixtures overhead.

Well-versed in both Christianity and Buddhism, **John Cormier** has served as a small-group spiritual leader. His fields of interest are human psychology, spirituality, and fine arts. This is his first publication.

Scott Flinchum

The Canoe

The old man's skill with an oar was still unquestioned: his strokes were swift and definitive. The power his old arms generated was enough to get them moved off the bank and into the current with little wasted movement—no mean feat for any person half his age, let alone a man of eighty. But there were hidden stories in the tan, leathered skin of his hands, tales that told of countless hours in the Little Pigeon River-way: long days on the water as a boy not much older than his grandson who sat and watched the old timer work now; days spent searching for pirate treasure; lone quests undertaken to save fair maidens; perilous journeys to rescue fellow watermen from sirens calling from their treacherous rocky outposts; nights spent sleeping under the stars; eyes fixed heavenward, gazing up at celestial multitudes too numerous to comprehend—ghost lights as infinite as Abraham's lineage was said to be.

The old man saw all these things in his mind's eye moving like an inner zoetrope—rushing years like a spinning axis, where each turn of the wheel added a new number to his individual chronology and subtracted additional tomorrows from his personal tally sheet. All these recollections were little more than a flash that faded with each stroke of his oar.

All of his youth and young manhood had passed in a similarly instantaneous manner as far as the old man was concerned. Even his middle years had seemed to move with the propulsive force of some untended rocket being shot into a void from which return was not just unlikely but preposterous to consider. He knew about such things—the unlikelihood of survival—because he had been in the business of combat for the majority of his working life. He had devoted himself to a definitiveness of thought, of action. Death had been his life's work.

What time he had been given was not enough from his perspective—would never be enough. Still, he remained thankful for the time he had had, the life he had led. By his own reckoning there wasn't much more of it he would be afforded: each second was a precious gift that he aimed to unwrap and use before the unseen claws of death took hold of him for good—which is exactly why he was on the water now: to put what good he had left in him to some use.

"I'm going to tell you a story. It's a tale from my youth. It's not a nice story…the most interesting ones never are."

His movements had slowed considerably now. The pass of his oar through the water less workmanlike, more contemplative now—as if movements could be said to hold within themselves the quality of the person enacting them, which, by the old man's measure, they certainly could, otherwise how could you explain the foresight an animal had when you turned your gun hand just so? Or, a person, for that matter?

The boy watched him from out of a trance: the rhythmic motions of his grandfather's arms—hairy, save for the barren patches of alien-looking, white keloid scars that decorated them—were moving in time with the burbling current. Each stroke of the oar as it sliced through the water appeared to the boy to be moving aside in deference; his grandfather like a living Moses reborn, giving the Red Sea a bit of a nudge so as to halve itself that much quicker for the coming of the Lord's wrath.

The strangeness of that thought and the image of the old man—whose wild thinning gray hair stood in all directions as the wind passed over it—made him want to laugh. He opened his mouth to do just that but was surprised to find that he couldn't manage it. In fact, it was hard to do much more than turn his eyes up to the old man's pinched and wrinkled sun-blotched face.

The boy blinked heavy-lidded eyes up at this fey boatman, feeling as if he were dreaming but somehow aware he was not. A torpor laid over him for which he could not account. The two of them drifted along—a lone craft on a Stygian tributary.

His grandfather had roused him from a nap a short while ago. He may have only been twelve, but he was not prone to napping. His mind felt muddled now. It wasn't unpleasant exactly, just…different. He also seemed to be curiously aware of his body—the ghost-like twitching of his limbs, the gauzy vision, the sound of his heart that thrummed in his ears like an out-of-sync cycle on a washing machine. He lingered over this last thought. He imagined the corpuscles that made up his blood as tiny articles of clothing spinning around inside him. Once again, he attempted to laugh. He still couldn't manage it.

"Now this story I'm about to tell you," his grandfather's voice said, sounding at once near and far away, "is from before your father was born.

It's from before the town you live in now grew up to the curious concrete scar that it's become."

The old man picked his oar up from the water and seemed to relax. He took in their surroundings—the dark water, the muddy banks, the herd of lowing cattle that patrolled the fence line on a nearby field. All of it felt familiar. Peaceful. Then he remembered why he was out here, and took up his story again with a grimness of the recently condemned.

"Most of it was still river bottom and forest," he called over his shoulder to his grandson, "with mountains propped up over all of it." He grunted and then set the oar in motion once again. "Now the river's polluted. The forest has been *developed* as they say. Them mountains," he said, briefly taking the dripping oar out of the water to waggle it towards collapsed-looking rock spires far in the distance, "have million-dollar homes perched on top of them."

The old man paused to look over his shoulder. The boy looked as docile and placid as the cows languidly staring at them from behind their rusted wire boundary. He kept the wooden tool in his hands working through the water as he watched his grandson. "It's a damn shame is all I'm saying."

The boy blinked. The slow crawl of his lids' closing momentarily broke the glossy-eyed stare that held the old man in front of him. A thin line of drool had begun to form at one corner of his half-opened mouth. The old man nodded as if the boy had agreed with him, then turned back to his work and the telling of his tale.

"The last I'd seen of this place was in nineteen hundred and sixty. As soon as I turned eighteen, I went downtown—wasn't more than a couple traffic lights and ten or twelve buildings at that time—and marched my way into the recruiting center. Got my physical, filled out my paperwork, and signed on the dotted line." He picked his oar up again and took in a deep lungful of air. "Shipped me off in eight weeks—which was shorter than they had been doing for basic training—and went di-rect to Viet-nam."

The boy moaned.

The old man glanced over his shoulder again. He scowled.

The boy's dark eyes tracked him. He tried to moan again but found it hard to muster the energy it required. The old man turned away once more, likely realizing the same thing. He passed his oar to the opposite side of the canoe. "Won't be too long now son…" The old man's words had softened. "…may have given you more than I intended. For that," he half-turned and flapped a hand behind him, "I'm sorry." He shifted back around to better navigate a half-submerged tree. "Had to be done though…had to be."

In a few short, deft movements, the old man set them back on a clear course. He paused, lifted the dripping oar onto his lap and took up where he had left off with the boy. "Where was I…ah, Viet-nam. I spent the better part of fourteen years entrenched in one way or another over there before that jabbering tit Nixon called the whole thing off in seventy-three. Bastard didn't know his ass from a—" He turned back to the boy and gave the child an apologetic wave. "Listen at me. Your grandmother would have my balls in some kind of vise if she heard me cursing around you—"

The old man's expression suddenly darkened. A cloud seemed to have passed over the shadowed sockets of his eyes—two gray orbs that seemed to be floating in tears yet to be shed. When he spoke again, his voice was just above a whisper and hard to make out over the sound of the fast-moving water as it cascaded and swept along the underside of the canoe. "You and I both know she ain't around now though son, is she?"

The boy attempted to speak. This time he managed a queer burbling sound from the collection of saliva that had amassed in his throat. The old man cradled his chin as if to consider this, then, satisfied, nodded at the boy once more as if he had spoken some infallible truth. He took up the oar and went back to his story.

"Before that prick Nixon came along, before Johnson, or even that playboy Kennedy got his head blown off, I was half a world away hunting men in rice patties and chasing them through the most god-awful jungle a twisted mind could conjure up." The old man paused, then added, "Maybe yours could…"

The old man didn't finish this thought. He leaned forward and scanned the horizon. He called behind him and gestured to where he had been looking. "It's just ahead now. I'll try and hustle this along but," he shrugged, "you know how old men get to talking…"

The old man used the oar like a rudder. He angled them around a large rock this time that jutted out from underneath the water. "What I'm saying is, I had to learn to hunt those men. My platoon leader told me when I first got over there and he started training me up, that I didn't have to like what I was doing, I just had to learn how to do it. Truth was though," the old man let his head drop down between his sharply angled bony shoulders, his eyes searching the water for something that he didn't seem to expect to find,

"I got to where I did like it. Loved it, if I'm honest."

The boy managed a louder sound. Along with this came the sudden brief sensation of movement in his fingers. His grandfather didn't turn around. He just nodded in his customary way as if his grandson's groaning was the boy holding up his end of the conversation. The old man raised his head back up and went back to slicing through the water.

"I'm not proud of it. But it's true. There were nights I'd lay awake on patrol, just praying—actually praying—for one of them Ho Chi Minhers to try skipping through our camp. I got to where I craved the combat. The killing." He shook his head. "Things were like that for damn near the entire first year I was over there. Hung around even during two-leave spells. But that second year, something shook me loose."

He turned and looked at the boy. His grandson looked back impassively from underneath heavily drooping lids. "Got me back on track is what I mean to say." The old man grunted as he shifted back around and swept the oar forward.

To the boy, his grandfather working that oar no longer reminded him of Moses. The old man seemed more like a Warlock brewing a curious mix of devilry in the waters of the Little Pigeon River. It felt as if he'd unexpectedly fallen into a dream rather than out of one. He'd gone headlong through some sinister creature's trapdoor into a demented fairy tale. For the first time in his young life, he felt just a tinge of what he imagined most normal people felt—a thing they called fear.

"When I started that second year," the old man's voice started up again, "the remaining guys from my platoon fell in with what was left of another group that had been nearly wiped out by the Vietcong. My captain oversaw the coming together of the two. There was a kid—and when I say kid I mean it—had to of lied on his draft papers cause there wasn't a chance in hell that boy was older than fifteen." He glanced again over his shoulder at the boy. "He barely looked older than you." He shifted his eyes forward and guided their vessel back into the current.

"This boy was green as an unripe tomato but the sweetest, kindest soul I ever met...til your grandmother came along." The old man's voice cracked. The boy couldn't see his grandfather's face but knew the old man must be hurting. He could remember the deep wrinkles his grandfather wore—those deeply carved lines, as if God himself had taken a knife to the old man.

"Less than a few hundred feet now son."

There was a warble in the old timer's intonations now. With a detached sort of interest, the boy watched the old man's shoulders hitch up and down for a time. *He's crying*, the boy thought, in nervous amusement.

"Let me finish this up quick," he said, as he sniffed back a string of tenacious sounding snot, "that boy took a turn with me on patrol just a few nights into his joining up with our group. I was my usual self—which was to say itching like a wino needing a slug, just praying for Charlie to pop up out of them deep jungle fronds—when it happened."

The old man slipped the oar back into the water and brought it around in a few deftly maneuvered half-arcs. He brought the canoe to rest directly in the center of a jumble of rocks as jagged as a ruined set of teeth. Their wooden craft now sat partially suspended in this natural lock. Once the old man was satisfied that they were cradled securely in their semi-enclosed chamber, he took the oar out of the water and set it beside him with a final flourish before shifting completely around to face the boy.

"We're here," he said. The old man's jaw gradually set, revealing the muscular pulley system underneath the thin skin of his wasted-looking face. There was a grim finality in his grandfather's features. Even in the state the child was in, the boy began to understand what this now was. Whatever the old vet had planned, his grandfather aimed to see it through. Neither heaven nor hell would stand in his way. His grandmother had made that clear a few times when he had played his game with her. She had spoken the old man's name like an invocation, as if the simple act of speaking it would be enough to make him materialize right there in that dank root cellar. It hadn't been. But she had told him plainly that his grandfather would bring hell down on him.

A sharp surge of fear unexpectedly thrummed through the boy like a circuit newly connected. He let out another groan, this nearly twice as loud as the other previous attempts; and, along with that, there was a sudden rush of feeling in both his hands and feet now. He started to move them but for reasons he could not immediately explain he managed to stop himself—he didn't want his grandfather to see.

The boy trusted in his instincts: they were what separated him from everyone else; they were how he managed to do what he did; they had helped him start to turn into what he felt he was becoming—what he was meant to be—something his grandfather had somehow become aware of.

How the old man had known about his wife, the boy's grandmother, what had happened to her, what the boy had done *to* her afterwards, he could only guess. But there was no doubting that his grandfather knew. That novel feeling—the fear—bloomed larger inside him.

"I know," the old man said as if reading his grandson's mind, "you're feeling it now...the fear. Probably the first time you've felt such a thing, I suspect." He grunted as he shifted on his bow seat. "I'll make this last part quick then...I probably ought not to, for what you done..."

The old man laced his fingers together and paused, seemed to regard them from some faraway perspective as he collected his thoughts, then dove back into the telling of his tale. "I took that boy on the same route I walked every patrol. We didn't just go to the defined perimeter of the camp," the old man shook his head miserably. "No, we damn sure went well beyond that. All because of me. All because I was hungry for some action—some blood."

His grandfather clenched his hands together so tightly they flared a spectral white to match his beard and his pale scars. "I had to have another kill—another notch on the tally sheet. I wasn't as sick with it as some of the poor bastards I ran across over the course of those years fighting." The old man cocked his head to one side and chewed at the side of his cheeks, seeming to debate some newly birthed thought. "Probably, they was just as vile and twisted as I suspect you are—or will be, given enough time..."

An osprey screeched overhead. The old man paused to watch it fly by. It carried a fish, freshly caught, water and blood dripping off the thing in turns from between the bird's talons. The fish's head was pointed forward in that curious way that ospreys are known to tote their kills—the bug-eyed osteichthyan given a front row seat to its own demise.

The boy did not see the animal as it flew past: his eyes remained fixed on his grandfather. Watching. Waiting.

The old man turned back to his grandson after the bird was lost to sight. He reached up and tugged on the lobe of one ear. The old man's eyes grew comically wide as he picked his story back up from where he had abruptly left it. "These were the type of guys who collected ears off the dead—their dead. Men. Women. Children. Everyone they killed. They'd wear 'em on homemade necklaces. With the heat and the sun, over time them wretched things would turn black and gnarled as banded cow balls." The old man made a sour face and cast his eyes down to where the oar rested on the badly scuffed floor of the canoe. "There's no doubt you'd be one of them types—or are one of them types. Brings me no satisfaction to say that son, but..." the old man threw up his hands, "there it is. It's said."

The boy's entire body seemed to have thrummed back to life. His awareness of his surroundings had increased as well. He could feel the drool working its way down his chin but he fought the urge to swipe at it. It was only a matter of time, he thought, before he could marshal the energy to lunge for the old bastard.

The fear began to ebb in him. In its place was the familiar sensation of control. But it was more than that: it was an instinctual knowing that what he was went beyond the old man's reckoning. He didn't need a war to go hunting. He had all the game he needed right where he was, and no need of any of the old timer's thin justifications for killing. He took what he wanted; the setting had never mattered to him.

He had dreamed about taking the old man's life—the combat veteran, the Purple Heart owner, the so-called "ass kicker." The ultimate trophy. He hadn't decided when or how he would do it, just that he would. It was obvious that that time was now. Whatever remained of the fear burned off him. It was time for him to play again.

The old man, lost in his thoughts, came back around to his task. He finally released his hands which he'd been clutching as if in wrathful prayer. The blood was slow in returning to them: he had to shake them to hurry the process along. They remained a sickly shade of purple, the veins tortuous and distended, as he reached down and took the oar in his hands.

"That boy," he said, returning back to his story once again, "that boy went with me to the back of beyond. He went chasing what I was after. Blood. Blood was what I wanted. And that boy spilled his because of me."

Miniature waves slapped the side of the canoe as the old man fell silent. Insectile chatter started in earnest from the trees heavy-laden with leaves overhead. Two generations looked at one another from their bobbing wooden island. Time passed slowly. Neither seemed able to truly breach the gap of understanding what it was that had created the other. With a sigh, and a shake of his head, the old man broke the silence.

"A small regiment of the People's Army sprung up out of their hides and lit us up with everything they had. I took a few of them out, but not before they peppered that kid with enough lead to clip off one of his wings, most of a leg, and open his belly for him."

The old man's lips began to tremble. He clutched the oar tightly with both hands. "His guts was spilled out. Nothing but the smell of shit, blood, and the sour tang of jungle rot. Seemed like the second you got dropped into that shit soup of a jungle you'd have that stink on you. Figured the kid would've been long gone by the time I dragged him back to camp. But wonders never cease. The poor bastard wasn't just alive when we got back, he was talking. Screaming too, something awful." The old man shook his head in equal parts wonder and disgust. He frowned at the remembrance of the thing. The lines that ran over his face deepened so much that they connected and resembled a crude-looking topographical map where pain was the only destination in all directions.

"I come clean as soon as we got back. My commanding officer told it to me plain. The kid may have been alive then, but it wasn't gonna last. His squalling wasn't going to be doing us any favors either. The CO didn't want to waste what small amount of morphine we had on a kid that was soon to be KIA, bringing in more of the enemy with his caterwauling. So, it come to me to take care of it. My fault, my responsibility."

The boy's grandfather waggled the oar in front of him. "Now we've come to it, I might as well tell it plain to you: I had to mercy kill that boy. You understand, son?" He looked from the boy down to the oar in his hands. He let out a long sigh. "Why'm I telling you all this?" He brought his head up to the sky as he asked the question. Slowly, his eyes found their way back down to meet the boy's. "Probably because no matter what you may be, you're still my grandson. In a way, you're my fault. And your daddy ain't around. So, you're my responsibility too."

The old man bobbed his head back and forth on his bony shoulders as if weighing what he would say next before finally coming to a decision. "And because I suppose even a creature as pitiful as what you are—what you're becoming—deserves some measure of knowledge about why they've gotta be blotted out. I gave up on God long ago to sort out His own ledger. That's what men are for in the end, I guess: to clean up His mess. 'You're mine, and I aim to settle things up 'fore I see my way out.'"

The old man slowly got to his feet. He had to stop several times on his way up to maintain his balance. He steadied himself with the oar as the minor wake he made from his standing rocked the vessel.

Once it passed, he took up the oar with both hands and held it aloft. It made him look like a lonely letter "T"—something that might come up on a demented children's show. There was a deadly calm that had swiftly settled

84

over the old man's wizened face. It was final. The hand of death extended.

"There's worse places to die, son," he said. "Like a jungle. Or," he paused, seemingly looking through the boy back to the memory of a life that had been and the person whom he had spent most of it with, "at the bottom of a root cellar. Like you done to her—your own grandmother."

The boy's face betrayed nothing. Not shock, not remorse. Whatever the old man had gotten into his system felt to have mostly worn off. The fear was little more than a vague recollection now. The boy felt he could take the old man. But he wasn't completely sure of it; at least, not enough to attack preemptively. He wanted his grandfather closer before he tried something like that.

As if tuning into the boy's own wavelength, his grandfather took a tentative step forward. He balanced himself using the oar above him. "I didn't expect you to say nothing. Pretty much saw to it that you wouldn't be able. But I want you to listen 'fore I end it. Before I do what God don't seem fit to do. I know she ain't the first you've done this to, my Linda. There've been others: vagrants…migrant workers—I'm guessing you bagged some of them. People probably chocked it up to natural causes, or accidents, or who knows what all. Or maybe you disappeared 'em so nobody would find 'em. Did you play with them? Their bodies? Like you done with her. My Linda." He took another step. He was near enough now that if he wanted to, he could have stretched out and tapped the boy with the leading edge of the wooden oar. "How many was it you done in?" he asked.

The boy said nothing.

"Five? Ten? More?"

The old man took two halting, shuffling steps forward. He loomed over the boy now, his leathery hands holding fast to the oar. In the late afternoon sun, with his shadow spreading long across the bow of the canoe, he called to mind an enchanted tree newly erupted from the planks of their vessel—as if he had been planted in that exact spot, growing upwards through the years in preparation for this moment.

"How a boy," the old man's voice boomed above him, "a child of twelve years old, can do the things you done…" The old man trailed off as he searched for the words to describe his grandson. "You're not just a freak. You're evil, son. You understand? Plain evil."

The boy's eyes rolled slowly up to find the old man's face. His lips parted and for a second the old man thought the boy would speak. Instead, a wan smile slipped over the child's face.

"You little—"

Hate flared up in the old man, sudden and uncontrollable. With a vicious swing he brought the oar around in a wide arc and then thrust it down towards the boy.

As he braced himself for contact, he realized something was wrong: the boy had moved—he wasn't where he should have been. He had somehow leapt forward.

A dark shape rushed at him. He looked down in time to see the crown of the boy's skull as it connected with his chest. A distorted cracking sound echoed over the water. The oar flew out of his hand. The old man let out a surprised cry as he tumbled backwards with the child on top of him.

As he fell, the boy's grandfather felt something rip and separate in his back. A flare of intense pain like internal heat lightning sprung to life along his left arm as he connected with one of the jagged rocks that surrounded the small, natural lock.

The two of them went flailing end over end into the water of the main channel. They splashed under. The pair of them gasped in unison as the cold murky water buffeted them further beneath the surface.

The old man felt the child's small hands clasping his neck. He struggled against the boy, realizing the severity of his injuries in that moment, how weak he had suddenly become. He felt as if his chest had cracked, his spine had broken, and the important muscles and ligaments surrounding his arm had been unceremoniously severed. If the child won though, there'd only be more killing—of this, the old man was assured.

Marshaling what remaining strength he had, he wrested the boy's hands free and used the base of the rocks to twist himself around enough to take the child's back. The boy was too late in realizing what was happening. He had been too fixated on finishing off his grandfather to reckon with one simple truth: his grandfather had given up on the idea of preserving his own life.

The boy thrashed. For a moment, the child thought he was free. He had managed to work his head briefly out of the water. He screamed. He did not cry for help. He just screamed like some feral creature. He screamed until his head slid back underneath the surface of the water. His grandfather drew him back down into his arms.

The boy flailed out and latched onto the oar before he went back down. As the pair sank further into the murk, the old man took hold of the oar and used it to help pin the two of them down among the rocks. With what remained of his strength, he leveraged the oar into a position where he could use it to better pin his grandson against him. The boy thrashed, but his grandfather held on.

The old man's skill with an oar was unquestioned: he drew it tighter against them. It was enough to hold them under—to do the job. They stayed that way—locked together—until the opalescent tracks of light that rippled over the surface of the disturbed water quieted. They stayed there until all faded to black: one final story told by the old man's scarred and leathery hands; one last kill; a hidden tale to join the discarded arrowheads and pieces of broken pottery on the river bottom; two more lives to be forgotten in the roiling tumult of time.

Scott Flinchum is a writer who currently resides in Southwest Virginia with his wife and children.

Lindsay Schlegel

Cheers to Fifty Years

Sandra couldn't see her husband pull the sedan into the driveway, but she heard him. In the passenger seat, she knew, lay the cake she'd ordered from the Italian bakery—half a vanilla sheet cake filled with cannoli cream and tiny chocolate chips, with cornflower blue roses made of buttercream on top, the color her bridesmaids had worn. In the rear footwells lay platters of cold-cut sandwiches and wraps stuffed with mayonnaise-based salads. David had argued that Sandra's cooking was far superior, but his flattery couldn't compensate for a pair of arthritic hands. She never thought she'd see the day when what could seem a loss of independence would feel like relief. Yet here it was.

They had discussed the details of their fiftieth anniversary party over a week's worth of dinners. Having lived in this house for as long as they'd been married, they didn't have much left to decide. Sandra wrote out the familiar guest list, hung the decorations, and spent the week before deep cleaning the entire house, save the attic. David rose early that morning to mow the lawn, shower, and run the list of errands laid out for him. There might have been more joy in managing their house, but now laundry, dishes, grocery shopping was just the next thing you did in a day.

Sandra heard David laugh from the driveway, the deep, throaty sound she'd fallen in love with decades upon decades ago. Now, an omen.

She stepped to the window in her stocking feet and saw David on his phone. He leaned against the tail end of the car effortlessly, the way he used to when he picked her up for a date. She cursed her stomach for twisting itself into an invigorating knot.

This was impossible half an hour before the party started. The car's passenger door stood open, forgotten. Without making out the words, she recognized a lift in the tone of his voice that sounded in her ears like a smoke detector, a car alarm, a tornado warning, though Sandra had never heard one of these last ones herself, living her entire life in a twenty-mile radius in the center of New Jersey.

Karen Dottingham had moved away a long time ago. She had not received an invitation.

Sandra forcibly opened the drawer of the sitting room hutch, bracing herself for the torrent of memories unearthing fifty years' worth of family portraits would yield. She imagined the pictures embroidered into the depths of her innermost being, the essence of why it was relevant that she existed in the world.

David still hadn't come inside. The ice was in a cooler in the trunk, melting. That laugh again, that Sandra had loved and then learned to let go of.

The kitchen door opened and she heard David's voice from the next room. "It was kind of you to call. Give Stephen my best."

Gingerly, for fear her shaking hands would bobble the frames and shatter the glass on the hardwood floor, Sandra propped up their wedding photo, housed in a Lenox frame embossed with the words "Forever and a Day." She flanked it with one of the twins ages ago on their first day of kindergarten on the left, and another of Mark with his wife, Beth, and their girls at the beach last summer on the right. She aligned the photographs using the lace doily beneath them as a guide.

"Hey, hon?" David called from the kitchen. "You want these out or in the fridge?"

Sandra's arms crossed over her middle. The dress she'd worn to her great niece's wedding last year pulled more tightly around her waist than she remembered. She'd spent an inordinate amount of time trying to decide if the lilac gown was too fancy—she was in her own house, for crying out loud—but Beth insisted it was her day.

It was silly for a woman of her age to care whether she looked like anything. Silly, silly. The word repeated in her mind. A word she used more these days because of their grandchildren. Silly. Silly.

"Sandra?" David called again. He leaned through the doorway. "The sandwiches?"

She didn't raise her eyes. "The counter is fine. There's a space for them."

He'd turned to go back into the kitchen when she said, "I'm going out for a while."

"What did you forget? I can run out again."

"How did she get your number?"

"Sorry?"

"Who was that on the phone?" Sandra said.

"Karen heard through the grapevine it was our anniversary. She wanted to tell us congratulations." No hesitation. He didn't have the decency to blush.

She thought she was nodding, until she recognized with clarity that her field of vision wasn't shifting.

"You ought to put the cake in the fridge. The frosting will wilt. Take it out at four so it's not too hard when you serve it," she said.

"Right. That's still in the car."

She didn't move until he'd gone back outside. Then she went upstairs, changed out of her dress and into a worn v-neck t-shirt and walking shorts. She added a nightgown and a few items from the bathroom to the tote bag she took to book club on Thursdays. In the foyer by the front door, she pulled the extra set of keys from the drawer and took her purse from its hook.

When David was bringing the last of the food inside, she slipped into the driver's seat and pulled away, leaving him to explain this time.

#

It had been so many years since Joanie—the only daughter, the twin sister—had died in a car crash that everyone else managed to survive. More or less. Mark coped with drugs, until his guidance counselor strongly suggested he switch schools. Cross-country and track teams replaced his nighttime wanderings and gave him the idea of a scholarship somewhere far, far away. Sandra told herself he was so focused he didn't see that his parents didn't talk anymore, that more and more often Dad wasn't home for dinner, that Mom was eating less and less.

Across the street, in a mirror image of the same colonial-style house, the Dottinghams were raising their four children. There was talk that Karen's husband welcomed the travel he did for work because things weren't good at home. Sandra listened to the playground gossip, curious what it looked like from the inside when "things weren't good."

The affair started Mark's senior year, Joanie's third anniversary. Why then, Sandra could never figure out. She learned to speak the language of household chores with fluency. Dishes could communicate aggression, piles of laundry shouted anxiety, a full garbage can left unemptied in a nearly dark kitchen at midnight said, "I am not as stupid as you think."

David began to whistle on Saturday mornings, when he did odd jobs around the house. Sandra hadn't registered the silence until there was something to replace it. He started to bring her coffee in bed, and didn't say anything when it was still beside her, cold, when Mark got home from an afternoon meet. He took it back downstairs, rinsed the mug clean, left it in the sink.

Mark was accepted to USC. Around the same time, Karen's husband got a new job, one that didn't require so much time away from his family.

David stopped whistling and Saturday morning repairs. He worked harder at the office, under the guise of retiring early. Hinges squeaked. Paint chipped. When enough broken things accumulated, Sandra hired someone to come and fix them all. She had the living room repainted, the basement carpet ripped out and replaced with something she was guaranteed wouldn't show a stain.

They played their roles well enough. At USC, there were parents' weekends, a girlfriend, then a fiancée, a wedding at her family's home in Connecticut. If nothing else, they looked like a family. Mark's life went on and allowed Sandra to press the reset button on her own. Never did she expect someone else to hit rewind.

#

It felt foolish to spend eighty-nine dollars plus taxes and fees to sleep just a few miles from home, but the Best Western the next town over had a vacancy, and Sandra got the AARP discount.

The embarrassing exchange at the front desk replayed in Sandra's mind as she slipped the key card in and out of the lock four times, trying to gain entry to her room.

Yes, party of one, she had confirmed with the receptionist, a disinterested younger woman (but who wasn't these days) with an off-center bun and a blazer that pulled across her chest. And yes, Sandra had assured her, she was familiar with the area.

Finally the swipe met whatever criteria lived inside that little box, and the green light turned on. She grunted as she pushed down on the handle and shoved the door open. How long had it been since anything had come easily to her?

She laid her bag on the closer of two identically dressed beds in a tidy, well-lit room she hadn't had to create for herself. Mini fridge, empty. A small notepad with the illegible impressions of the last guest's thoughts. A television too big for the space, a remote with too many buttons at its side.

Sandra sat in the swivel chair at the desk and tried to figure out what she was doing. Hiding? Shaming? Leaving? Whatever it was, there was one thing she had to take care of.

She pulled out her phone and dialed Mark.

Beth answered. "Hi, Sandra. We're in the car, on our way."

"I'm sorry to do this, dear, but I'm afraid I'm not feeling well. You ought to stay home today."

"Mom?" Mark said. "What's going on?"

"We'll just have to find another time to celebrate."

"Is Dad okay?" Mark asked.

"Are you calling everybody? Is there something we can do?" Beth asked.

"How about we plan to see you next weekend?" Sandra said. "I think that would be best."

Beth started to ask something else, but Mark spoke first.

"Feel better, Mom."

"Thank you, sweetheart. Give the girls my love."

Sandra turned her phone off after she hung up. She could imagine the conversation Mark and Beth were having right now, trying to decide whether to follow her order. She felt badly putting them in that position, and had to remind herself—again—that it wasn't really her fault.

A cranberry-colored binder advertised notable attractions, most of which were in New York City. A lifetime ago, it would have been a dream come true to play at a more glamorous version of herself. The older she got, the more crowds nauseated her. She could barely watch the Thanksgiving Day parade on television anymore.

She unpacked her toothbrush and toothpaste and made sure her room key—one of two, she wasn't sure why—was tucked away in her bag. When she took in her reflection in the full-length mirror, her shoulders involuntarily pushed themselves back, her tummy sucked itself in. This wasn't the woman she had intended to become.

She turned away before exhaling into a minor but well-established slump.

"Well. That's settled then," she said out loud. With some effort, she pulled the door open.

The latch might have echoed if it hadn't been for the thick carpeting in the corridor, the plush wall coverings that swallowed up the slightest sound.

#

In the lobby, Sandra intended to take herself to the bar and boldly order a cocktail. She'd never drunk alone before, and it seemed to be what a Meryl Streep character would do if she were in this situation. The click of her low heels fell away as she crossed from the tile floor of the lobby into the carpet of the restaurant. The oxygen disappeared in the few epic moments she waited for a bartender to appear. Before he could, she was in her car, gasping for breath, her heart rate slowly returning to normal.

She resolved to try again and walked down the block to a sparsely decorated coffee shop. She ordered a *café au lait*, because it sounded exotic, and opened her book for book club, which was pitched to the group as "life-changing." Even with coffee, she couldn't concentrate.

She didn't expect David to make a confession when he would have proposed a toast. It wasn't as if he were the first man to cheat on his wife. She wasn't the first woman to stick around.

She'd wanted to be married in the fall for the vibrant colors of the trees. Later, she thrived on the stark contrast of a crisp morning and a cozy dash of cinnamon in hot coffee while she waited for the bus with the kids. Tears muddled her gaze onto the sidewalk now, as she flipped through mental images of dates with David at the local diner, where they'd talked until their milkshakes grew warm or their coffee got cold. That laugh that sounded like heaven. Their careful selection of interior paint colors, refinishing furniture from yard sales to save a buck, each element of their house so carefully placed to create a home. Years of infertility, and then—surprise!—twins as some sort of cosmic bargaining for their suffering. Each time she looked into their babies' faces she saw living, breathing evidence that she and her dear David could weather anything.

Exhaustion from the double-dose of colic, flu seasons, stomach bugs, soccer practices. Everything for the twins. Vacations down the shore, and then darkness. Pain that hollowed her out, that tore the family to pieces. Proof that she had not, in fact, worked hard enough to bind her family together. The question plagued her, but she'd never been able to say it out loud. What in the world could she have done better? Something? Everything? Or, what was worse, was it all really out of her control?

It started to get dark, and more people came into the shop. One set up a small speaker and a guitar at the far end. Sandra left her table and ordered soup, a sandwich, and a brownie to go. Back at the hotel, she fell asleep to the eleven o'clock news after watching a movie she'd seen bits of before, but she'd never learned its name.

#

In the morning, Sandra showered and ironed the only shirt she'd brought. She dressed, pulled the covers back into place, and left a tip for the maid.

"I've made my point," she said, assessing herself in the mirror. And then again, more loudly, "I've made my point."

She drove the short distance home—no map app needed—and imagined what she'd find. David's side of the closet cleaned out, a note saying he just couldn't live a lie anymore. Or maybe he'd be fixing the leak under the kitchen sink that she'd left a note about weeks ago. It was unlikely he'd have cleaned up the fallout from the party, put the furniture back in place, stowed the Saran-enrobed leftovers in the fridge. He could figure out how to run the vacuum if he tried.

She hadn't turned her phone back on since calling Mark. At the front door, she debated which terrifying thing to do first. All she needed to know was whether David was home.

She stepped into a room decorated with balloons, some hovering at the ceiling, others standing at half-mast. She'd intended to give the good ones to their granddaughters at the end of the party.

David sat in his customary spot, an opened but otherwise untouched beer bottle on the coaster beside him. He looked up from a DVR recording of yesterday's USC football game, but remained in his chair.

She wished she could be certain that the painfully nostalgic sting of citrus in the air was what brought tears to her eyes. The bit of red at David's lip might be ketchup or a nick from shaving, though he hadn't done that this morning.

"You're back," he said.

"I never intended to stay away. I just wanted to . . . I needed . . ."

94

"I looked like a fool. What was I supposed to say?" He leaned forward in his chair, his shoulders tensed, his eyebrows pulled together to emphasize the belittling tone.

Sandra hadn't put her bag down yet. She clutched it now, standing like a schoolgirl accepting a scolding. Wasn't the bag's compactness proof enough?

"Mark and Beth and the girls didn't come," he said.

"I told them not to."

"I thought you wanted to have this party," David said.

On the hutch, the photo of the twins had been put away, the other frames adjusted to create their own display.

He closed his eyes. "Nothing happened."

"Yesterday or then?"

He sighed dramatically, as if all this was beneath him. "We all did things we shouldn't have. We all fell apart."

"It doesn't make it okay. It was never okay."

The doorbell rang, followed by a quick double knock, Mark's signal.

Sandra opened the door, her bag still in her hand.

"Hey, Mom. Sorry the party fell through."

"Thank you, dear," Sandra said, accepting his hug.

"Beth and I wanted to see how you were feeling." He looked toward the car. Beth waved. Sandra waved back.

"You didn't answer your phone," Mark said.

"I forgot to turn it back on," Sandra said.

He looked down at her hands. "You on your way out somewhere?"

"I'm just coming home," she said.

Mark's eyes roamed the room. A handful of used paper plates and plastic cups rested on various horizontal surfaces. A crushed chip lay at his feet. His expression grew slack, his eyes moved from one parent to the other.

"We wanted to give you this." He handed Sandra a creamy envelope, bursting with its contents. "Happy anniversary."

Sandra nodded. "Thank you, honey. And tell Beth the same."

"Give the girls our best," David said.

Mark shook his head. "We're all adults now, so I can tell you this. You're both horrible liars."

The room was silent in a way that seemed unbreakable, the way it was after Joanie died, when they came back from the hospital and for days, no one had anything worth saying.

Mark had let himself out. Sandra looked down at the envelope. She gently pulled the flap free and took out a card with generic sentiments about love and eternity, a bonus "Congratulations!" in Beth's easy script.

"They want to send us on a cruise in the spring. Alaska," Sandra said.

David nodded. "Very generous. Fishing."

"Sunsets. Cold."

"I didn't get you anything," David said with a shrug of shoulders that were beginning to turn in on themselves.

"You should have," she said quietly. He nodded and turned back to the television.

She walked upstairs, put her toothbrush and nightgown back in place. She laid the book by her bed, knowing she wouldn't read it. When she went back downstairs, the game was tied, the brochure still lodged within the card on the coffee table. Sandra took them into the kitchen and clipped the image of a huge boat in stunning blue water before an even more enormous range of purple snow-capped mountains to the calendar on the fridge.

She brewed a cup of coffee and sliced herself a piece of leftover cake for breakfast. The icing was still hard and tasted mostly of butter. Things had been put away, but not in the right places. She licked the last bit of a sugar rose from her fork, and then set about cleaning up.

Lindsay Schlegel is a freelance writer and editor, who has served in various roles in traditional publishing for nearly twenty years. Much of her editorial work concerns children's literature, while her writing is thus far mainly for adults. Her writing has appeared in *Verily*, *America*, *Word on Fire*, *The Windhover*, *Aleteia*, and more, both online and in print.

Lindsay is the author of _Don't Forget to Say Thank You: And Other Parenting Lessons That Brought Me Closer to God_ as well as the co-author of _The Road to Hope: Responding to the Crisis of Addiction_. She hosts the podcast _Quote Me with Lindsay Schlegel_, which is currently on hiatus while Lindsay pursues a Master of Fine Arts degree in creative writing at the University of St. Thomas, Houston.

She lives in New Jersey with her husband and their five children. Connect with Lindsay at her website, her Substack, or on Twitter or Instagram.

Ryanne Molinari

The Sacrifice

At the beginning of the year, Mrs. Mendall's sixth-grade class adopted a ferret. It spent a week being jostled in its cage by curious children until, one morning, a more intriguing object arrived: a glass tank illuminated by heat lamps, crawling with tubes and wires. Forgetting the ferret, the students gathered around the incubator with unprecedented orderliness, perhaps sensing the delicacy of its contents.

"Can I see?"

"Is that — ?"

"It couldn't be!"

"I heard they do a lab with a real — "

"That speck?"

"It could be!"

Speculation simmered, fluttering from the students' lips and hovering hot on the glass before fading to nothing. At the exact moment that the intercom sounded for class to begin, Mrs. Mendall strode into the room, welcoming her students as she tossed a half-empty paper cup into the wastebasket without looking. Cold coffee sloshed against the plastic lining. Her entrance and greeting were mechanical, the product of twenty years in the profession.

"Good morning, ladies and gent — " She caught herself: no archaic language. "Students," she finished instead.

The children scurried to their desks — all but one girl, who lingered by the tank. She stood so close that her nose left a smudge on its side that remained even when her breath died away.

"You'll have a chance to see inside the tank soon," said Mrs. Mendall.

"I can't see it," murmured the girl.

"That's alright." Mrs. Mendall consulted her tablet, which glowed with the faces and names of the students before her. "Bethany, is it?"

The girl nodded and adjusted her oversized glasses, which were nearly as opaque as the smudge on the glass. Mrs. Mendall's brow creased as she looked between the girl on her roll sheet and the girl before her, who had lost the healthy pinkness in that former girl's cheeks and lips. She would

97

speak to the school nurse later.

Mrs. Mendall resumed her clipped tone. "I'm surprised anyone can see what's in the tank. Do any of you know what it might be?"

Bubbling with rumors only minutes before, no student stirred now. Mrs. Mendall tried again. "Bethany gave us a good hint about what's in this tank. It's one of the smallest objects visible to the naked eye. Does anyone want to guess?"

The tank was hot under the scrutiny of twenty-seven pairs of eyes, all straining to see the impossible thing within. Finally, a red-haired child in the front volunteered. "Yes, Amelia?"

"Mel, please."

"Of course — " she made a quick note. "Mel?"

"Is it an egg?"

"You're close! It's a bit more than that. Does anyone know?"

Every student leaned forward, captivated by what they'd only discussed in whispers, blushes, and jokes, but that was now before them.

"Nobody?" Mrs. Mendall tsk-tsked. "And I was told you'd be my brightest sixth graders yet!"

Mel ventured, "It starts with a Z?"

"Good," said the teacher. "If you look at the screen, you'll see a magnified photo of what we have in this incubator: a fertilized egg, a zygote."

She swiped through slides. "You might have heard of this project from friends or siblings, so I hope you're excited about it. Can anyone tell me what they know about this project?"

A few hands waved in the air as whispers flit about the classroom. Mrs. Mendall smiled indulgently; this lab had always been popular. It had been conceived several years ago. After the pandemic, the district began cutting funding for art and other non essentials. With a newly-bloated S.T.E.M. budget, Sanger Elementary purchased updated science equipment, including a groundbreaking device: the Class Mother 2029 Artificial Womb.

A child in the front row raised his hand so high that it drew him up like a fish on a line. Another student coughed impatiently. Bethany coughed for real and her seatmate shot her a look of concern.

Mrs. Mendall called on the fishing line boy. "Yes?"

"This is the experiment where we get to see pre-birth development and we get to grow an actual — "

"Correct." Mrs. Mendall signaled for him to sit, cutting him free and dropping him back to his seat, breathless. "Thank you — ?"

"Evan."

"Of course. That's right, Evan." Mrs. Mendall proceeded to inform her students that, since they had spent a large portion of the previous year studying anatomy and were themselves growing by leaps and bounds, it was fitting to participate in a simulation of the reproductive systems in real-time. Flipping off the lights, Mrs. Mendall began to explain the workings of the Class Mother 2029.

The tank's contents glowed a fleshy hue, illuminating a heated, bag-like structure within. Some could even detect — veiled by the plastic womb — the faintest ghost of the CM2029's tiny ward.

―――――

Mrs. Mendall filled another cup with lukewarm coffee and sank gratefully into a seat opposite a younger teacher. The long hours on her feet were not as kind as they'd once been. Miss Williams, the younger teacher, smiled shyly. The older teacher considered her bright eyes and brighter cardigan. It had been several decades since Mrs. Mendall had been the new teacher, but she remembered the nerves that had sustained her through those first weeks. A rush of sympathy came over her — or perhaps it was the caffeine.

"How's your day going?" the younger teacher asked.

"Not bad," said Mrs. Mendall. "My students are a bright bunch, but I'm worried about one little girl . . . "

"Poor thing."

"I'll talk to the nurse," Mrs. Mendall went on. "How's your first month going?"

"Well," Miss Williams blushed, "jumping straight into a project as big as this one is intimidating, especially since . . . "

"Since?"

There was a catch in Miss Williams' voice. "My subject isn't viable. I'm not sure what happened, but I got an alert on the CM2029 this morning after the children left for Phys. Ed. There was some complication with the chromosomal alignment. Something didn't divide properly and I had to discard it."

The young teacher was nearly crying. Mrs. Mendall was taken aback but reassumed her brusque manner. "I wouldn't worry too much about it. Just send a lab order for another; they have a viability guarantee, you know."

"Yes, I know," Miss Williams sniffled.

"Order another. It'll be here soon."

Mrs. Mendall was on her feet a split second before the intercom sounded the end of lunch. Miss Williams rose too, pulling her cardigan tightly around her shoulders. "The kids were so excited about this one," she sighed. "They were already talking about names, whether it might be a boy or gi — "

"Order another," Mrs. Mendall said firmly. "Your students can observe ours in the meantime. Then they'll have a head start on the curriculum when your replacement arrives."

"Really?" Miss Williams brightened. "Thank you."

As they passed through the hall, Miss Williams slowed and the fog settled over her face again, a gloomy contrast to her sunny sweater.

"What?"

"Nothing," said Miss Williams. "It's silly."

"Well?"

"I don't know . . . " she hugged herself. "Part of me feels that I'm to blame and . . . that something died."

All sympathy vanished from Mrs. Mendall's face, replaced by a blank look, as bland as sleep mode on a smartboard. "Don't be silly. It wasn't your fault. Besides, nothing can die that was not really alive."

The intercom sounded its last, ending the conversation and sending both teachers to their classrooms, the younger apprehensively and the older mechanically. As the semester passed, the sixth-graders of Sanger Elementary School grew, but not enough to be noticed until picture day arrived to reveal the changes a year brings to children: bangs cut, braces removed, waists whittled. Such changes seemed enormous when old and new pictures were taped side-by-side on refrigerators but remained invisible during their evolution.

There were three exceptions to this rule, the first being Bethany. She grew paler and thinner every day. Insubstantial as mist, Mrs. Mendall feared the girl might be vaporized by a sudden breeze or too strong a breath. The other exceptions grew steadily within the Class Mothers, which continued to hum their mechanical lullabies. The first subject, in Mrs. Mendall's classroom, progressed with visible proclivity. The other, although a week behind, was developing with a smoothness that reassured Miss Williams.

"Second time's the charm," said Mrs. Mendall. "I've never seen one grow so rapidly."

"You mean it?" Miss Williams looked up from where she was hovering over the monitors.

"Of course. You'll explain nutrition soon, right?"

"Yes, that's the lesson plan for this week, as long as the tubes and catheter keep looking good . . ." she glanced at the older teacher for approval.

"Your subject wouldn't be developing so healthily otherwise," said Mrs. Mendall, emotionless as the monitor.

Miss Williams' shoulders relaxed even as she frowned.

"Maybe — " she faltered, "maybe that's why the first one didn't make it."

"Don't even say that," said Mrs. Mendall. "That was a chromosomal issue. It wasn't your fault and wasn't in your control. Even if it was, you have no reason to feel guilty. None."

Mrs. Mendall repeated under her breath: no reason for guilt. Miss Williams watched her face with concern. Noticing, Mrs. Mendall shrugged, straightened her blouse, and marched out.

"Coffee," she said in explanation.

Instead of going to the lounge, though, Mrs. Mendall turned back to her own classroom. She had twenty minutes before her students would traipse through the door, yawning as half-digested cereal and Pop-Tarts sat heavily in their stomachs. She glanced over the monitors on the CM2029 but avoided the curled figure within.

"Not your fault. No reason to feel guilty. No reason at all." Mrs. Mendall recited this litany to herself as she prepared her materials, inhaling the educational incense of sweat, hormones, and sterilized equipment. She then sank into her seat and drew open the metal drawer of her desk. It opened with a grating cry that set her teeth on edge. Forcing herself to unclench her jaw, she reached into the drawer, paused, and withdrew her hand: empty.

Barren.

A knock at the door startled her. She slammed the drawer shut and beckoned jerkily for the visitor to enter. The school nurse poked her rosy face inside.

"Oh!" she clasped her hands in delight. "Another incubator lab! Going well, I hope?"

"Very."

"I remember doing these projects in grade school, so many years ago . . . Back then, we did them with chicks, you see. They were the cutest things when they hatched, but were boring until then since all we could see were eggshells. You're lucky you can see this dear creature every step of the way! How wonderful for the children — "

As the nurse prattled on, Mrs. Mendall found that she was still gripping the drawer handle. Finger by finger, joint by joint, she forced herself to let go. Clucking like her remembered chickens, the nurse made her way to Mrs. Mendall and slid a note across the desk. "—I can only imagine what we would have thought of this project back in my days. It would have stunned us into studying, I'm sure."

Mrs. Mendall scanned the report. "This could have been an email."

"You're probably right," said the nurse, dropping the chatter. "But it's a sensitive case and I know you're concerned for the poor dear."

"It's that serious?"

"We don't know for sure yet, but I'll tell you honestly that I'm not hopeful." The bell once ended their conversation and ushered in twenty-six students when there ought to have been twenty-seven. So unassuming when present, Bethany's absence was noticed immediately by both adults. The nurse left with a final glance at the CM2029.

"I remember," she said. "One of our chicks didn't make it. It was hard to understand as a kid, but the shell hid everything so it wasn't too bad. I'm not sure why I thought of that. It's one advantage to the old lab, I suppose."

Eight weeks into the semester, Mrs. Mendall arrived to find her students clustered once more around the CM2029, Bethany at the heart of the group. She seemed to be shrinking at the same rate that the subject in the artificial womb was growing: at least a millimeter each day. Even at such a rate, the CM2029 seemed monstrous, inappropriately industrial for the delicate thing it cradled in the synthetic embrace of feeding and respiratory tubes.

"I still can't see it," sighed Bethany. She coughed into her sleeve.

"It's the size of a raspberry," said Mel. "That's what the homework said. And it'll be the size of a strawberry in two more weeks."

"What kind of berry will it be after that?" someone teased.

Amelia grew thoughtful. "I don't think there are any bigger berries."

"It looks like an alien," added another student. "Gross."

"All right, class," Mrs. Mendall said. "Go to your seats."

With that, the half-drunk coffee was in the wastebasket, and the teacher was in position at the front of the room. The students trailed to their desks, walking in time to the beeping of a new monitor. Bethany was the last to sit, but Mrs. Mendall did not hurry her as she lingered, trailing her fingers across the glass tank as if longing to caress the figure within, to know by touch what she could not by sight.

The teacher needed no help in directing her students' gaze to the incubator. They were enraptured by its berry-sized occupant. When asked if they noticed any new additions to the CM2029, more than a few raised their hands, Bethany included.

"A heart-rate monitor?" Bethany ventured. "It sounds like the ones they use at my appointments."

"That's absolutely right!" Mrs. Mendall awarded her a rare, real smile. "At this stage, we can not only detect a regular heartbeat but see the heart itself if you look closely enough, as many of you already have."

Just as Amelia predicted, the subject doubled in size over the next few weeks. By the time it was the size of a strawberry, Bethany exclaimed in delight, "Jane, I can see it!"

"Are you sure?" pressed Amelia.

"Yes, I can," breathed Bethany. "I can see the baby."

"Fetus," corrected Amelia.

"Whatever," said Jane, coming to stand beside her friend. "Isn't it beautiful?"

"It still looks like a lizard to me," said Amelia.

"It's just little," said Bethany, "but it's growing so fast."

An exclamation from across the hall caught their attention and the girls, forgetting their differences, rushed the door only to find their path blocked by Mrs. Mendall, holding her half-empty cup.

"Seats, please," she said as she tossed the cup and released the doorstop in one well-oiled motion. The girls stole one last look across the hall to where Miss Williams' door stood open and the young teacher hovered over a cluster of students like a hen with her brood.

"Yes, yes," she was saying, "and those are its toes! Can you see? Can you count them?"

Even from across the hall, there was a warmth in the younger teacher's voice that blew into their classroom, a final summer breeze cut off by the sharp click of the heavy door.

"Take your seats," said Mrs. Mendall again. "Switch on your e-readers and — yes, Bethany?"

"What was Miss Williams saying? I could hear — "

"We'll get to that later. As I was saying, please swipe to — " another hand interrupted. "Yes, Jane?"

"I heard something about toes. Does ours have toes? I didn't look." She nodded toward the form wrapped and pulsing behind glass, now the size of a lemon. "Does it have toes now, too?"

The class inched forward in their seats, textbooks still switched off or buffering. Mrs. Mendall sighed, perhaps wishing for her discarded coffee. She set aside her e-reader and reclined against her desk.

"Yes, ours has toes," she said. "But ours is a week older than Mrs. Williams' subject, so does anyone know what else it has?"

The students strained to see the thing nestled against the Class Mother's heat lamp breast. The clock ticked in syncopation with the heart rate monitor. "Anyone?" Mrs. Mendall let a few more seconds slip by before a student gasped and stood, sending his chair screeching backward as he lurched across his desk to peer into the incubator.

"Yes, Evan?"

"Ours has a face!"

The alarm sounded unexpectedly. Unphased, the students of Sanger Elementary filed outside, holding their ears or shouting to friends. They were glad to exchange the fluorescent chill of their classrooms for the morning sun. Their teachers followed, twirling lanyards like lassos and struggling to corral their students.

Mrs. Mendall and Miss Williams herded their classes onto the athletic fields. Miss Williams greeted the older teacher with a tense nod. Her knuckles were white, clutching her roll sheet anxiously.

"Didn't know we were having a fire drill today?"

Miss Williams shook her head. "It's just a drill? You're sure?"

"Most likely. That or someone overcooked their microwave meal again. Either way, there's nothing to worry about. You there! Knock it off!" Mrs. Mendall moved to separate a group of children, who were sending each other into hysterics by mouthing four-letter words with each blare of the alarm.

Miss Williams stared back at the school, where alarms continued to scream through the empty halls. She watched as if expecting smoke to billow from its roof, but all was still. Its barrenness was somehow more disconcerting.

"It's silly of me," she said as she began counting her students. "But I couldn't help worrying about the babies and I was afraid — "

"The what?" Mrs. Mendall looked at her colleague as if she were spewing profanities along with the students.

"Fetuses," amended Miss Williams. "I didn't feel right about leaving without knowing they were safe."

"They're fine," said Mrs. Mendall. "Frankly, I'd be more concerned about getting your students in order."

Miss Williams wilted. "You're right, sorry. I shouldn't have worried. How's your subject doing, by the way?"

"Fine."

"Oh, good. After my first had to be discarded, I was so anxious for this one, but he's doing well."

"He?"

"Oh, yes! The genitalia is pretty well-developed, and the students are thrilled. They had a bet going on whether it would be a boy or girl. Whoever guessed right gets a say in naming it."

Mrs. Mendall's lips disappeared into a line. From the distance, the intercom announced an all-clear. She said nothing as they herded their students back inside. "So, yours is . . . ?" Miss Williams attempted.

"XY as well."

With that, Mrs. Mendall swept her students inside. With the morbid attraction of picking a scab, she could not keep her eyes from the scrunched figure in the CM2029, nor could she erase from her memory the inexplicable pang she'd felt when the alarm sounded and the subject started in surprise. She could not forget the sudden, ridiculous impulse to soothe the tiny creature from its first fright.

That afternoon, for the first time in her professional career, Mrs. Mendall released her students early. They left hesitantly, unsure what had come over their teacher. When the door shut behind them, Mrs. Mendall collapsed behind her desk. Once more, she reached for the desk drawer. This time, she opened it and removed a black-and-white photograph in a simple frame. She held it tentatively, between her forefinger and thumb, as though afraid it might burst into flames. Suddenly, she broke into a sob but indulged this fit for only a moment. She switched off her tears as if she, too, were kept alive by mechanics.

Another fit — this time of coughing — erupted from behind the CM2029. Mrs. Mendall flinched, dropping the frame.

"Bethany," she cried, "what are you doing here?"

Still coughing, Bethany tried to answer as she fumbled on the floor for the frame. Her own frame shook violently, but she managed to say through a phlegm-muffled voice, "I'm sorry — Mrs. Mendall. Fire drills used to scare me — so I wanted — to make sure he was okay."

Holding the frame and steadying herself against a desk, Bethany squinted at its contents: a figure similar to the one in the CM2029. It was barely a silhouette, but it held the promise of the fullness of life.

"Is it yours?" Bethany whispered.

"He was," said the teacher.

Bethany nodded. With a shuddering breath, she rose and handed the frame to her teacher. Shouldering a backpack much too bulky for her emaciated shoulders, she looked lovingly at the occupant of the CM2029. Perhaps sensing her presence, it turned toward the warmth of her weak gaze. When she reached the doorway, Bethany paused to look back at her teacher with the same tender expression.

"Mrs. Mendall?"

"Yes, Bethany?"

"I'm sorry."

The nurse arrived in Mrs. Mendall's classroom with mouth and eyes running. She delivered the news that Bethany was not getting better. "She's not contagious. She wants to come to school as long as she can."

Half-listening, Mrs. Mendall began her routine checks of the CM2029. Marvelous machine, it did everything for her. She was outdated.

How long until the Class Mother 2029 became the School Teacher 2033? How long until she was a fossil, something to study in history lessons? A sense of foreboding folded around her, turning her mood sourer than ever. To make matters worse, the lounge was out of coffee. Suddenly, the even pulse of the heart-rate monitor seemed an affront. How dare something so lifelike grow within something so cold and lifeless when she couldn't — well, never mind that. But how horrible that organs within an artificial womb could function flawlessly while a fully-formed girl had to fight for every breath.

A phrase she'd read long ago swam before her eyes: "fearfully and wonderfully made." 'Wonderful' had always seemed a given. 'Fearful,' she now understood. Unable to drown such contemplations in lukewarm coffee, Mrs. Mendall steeled herself to teach one of the last lessons before she turned her classes loose to write their lab reports.

"We're still a few weeks from the conclusion of this lab, but we need to define the vocabulary that you'll need for your reports," she said. "The first term is what you'll use to refer to the subject. Does anyone know it?"

"Fetus?" Amelia offered.

"Technically, yes." Mrs. Mendall waited, but nobody else volunteered. She found herself looking expectantly at the empty seat beside Jane where Bethany should have been. Her eyes darted to the drawer containing the old photo in its frame.

She pressed on. "In the scientific community, there's another word for subjects like this. Mel, would you please read from section 279 in your textbook?"

As Amelia began reading, the door slammed open to reveal Miss Williams, frantically buttoning and unbuttoning the top clasp of her cardigan. Mrs. Mendall rushed over. After a whispered conference, she sighed and turned to her class.

"Miss Williams will be taking over for now. Behave." With that, Mrs. Mendall grabbed a sterile box from beside the CM2029, shot her students a menacing look, and darted across the hall.

When the teachers met again at lunch, Mrs. Mendall had a fresh coffee and seemed to have regained her composure since the morning.

"It's done?" Miss Williams asked, idling near the coffee pot.

"Nearly," replied Mrs. Mendall. "This new termination method takes longer, but it's easier clean-up."

"So now what?"

"You take it to the lab for preservation and bring back samples for your students to examine."

"I . . . take him?"

"You'll be fine. Did you ever do a rat dissection in school? Animal rights activists shut that one down, but it's the same idea and most of the same parts." Miss Williams nodded. "Well, thank you for performing the . . ."

"Sacrifice."

Miss Williams pulled her cardigan around her so that its threads protested audibly. "Yes, that. The sacrifice."

When Mrs. Mendall tossed her coffee cup in the bin the next week, it was empty. It bounced off the rim and into the corner but she paid it no heed. Most unusually, she had arrived ten minutes late.

Her students were clustered around the cage at the back of the room. The ferret, rumored to be pregnant, was once more a subject of popular interest. "Seats, please," Mrs. Mendall said, lacking her usual brusqueness. "I must tell you something . . ."

That their classmate was dead did not seem real. Didn't Mrs. Mendall know that twelve-year-olds were invincible? To all but Jane, it was just another news story. They adjusted their attitudes accordingly but Mrs. Mendall could see that the reality of Bethany's passing would not pierce their souls for some time. For now, the students would do what they could. Today, they would whisper at lunch. Tomorrow, they would wear Bethany's favorite color to show solidarity and to convince themselves that they believed what their teacher was saying: that, while yellow shirts might fill the halls, Bethany's seat would remain forever barren.

The day that everyone wore yellow was the final day of the lab for Mrs. Mendall's class. As with the first day, her students exchanged rumors mixed with truth — the most palatable kind — about what would happen to the subject in the CM2029. "I heard that — "

"Miss Williams' class had to end early."

"But what did they do?"

With each minute, their speculations grew more outlandish and, ironically, closer to the truth. Would it be given away like the ferret's offspring? Broken down for parts like robotics projects? Flushed away like fish won at carnivals?

Mrs. Mendall allowed her students to speculate as she scanned her roll sheet. She didn't need it to know who was missing, but it was interesting to see the class photos. Nine months wrought such stark changes on children. She called their names, hastening past the pregnant pause where Bethany's should have been. She took an extra moment to log attendance, breathing deeply to prepare for the labor before her. The final step of the lab had never bothered her much, but she was not as young as she once was. She was not as strong as she once was.

"I gather from your whispers that nobody read ahead in the textbook?" Twenty-six pairs of blank eyes met her gaze. A twenty-seventh pair fluttered its lids, dreaming whatever dreams might be had within a lifeless womb, a glass coffin. "I'll explain as we go." Mrs. Mendall pulled on a pair of antiseptic gloves ("How fitting!" she thought morbidly, "They're yellow.") She selected a syringe of fluid — also a sickly yellow — and attached a needle that sparkled wickedly under the fluorescent lights. For a moment, Mrs. Mendall became something from an old horror film. At any moment, she might have donned a blood-streaked lab coat and begun bellowing, "It's alive! It lives!"

But the progeny within the CM2029 was destined for another, less melodramatic fate. In a matter of minutes, the lab that had taken all year was finished. The needle penetrated the plastic womb and its occupant. It was then withdrawn, capped, and dropped into a biohazard receptacle. The monitors on the CM2029 slowed and the tank resealed with a whine like that of a wounded animal.

Stillness fell over the class. Nobody uttered a sound, not even Amelia. The students watched the subject fight for its first and last breath, its wet lips pursed for a first and final cry.

As the subject stopped writhing, Mrs. Mendall began her closing remarks. "Remember, students, in science as in life, we have choices. This is a gift, but also a responsibility. Even a viable subject like this one can be terminated if we choose. Do you remember the lab that we read about earlier this year? With the mice?" The class nodded.

"Do you remember what happened to those mice when the

experiment ended? What did the researchers do with them?"

"They were sacrificed," Amelia said, without her usual zeal.

"Exactly. And do you remember why it's called that?"

Amelia scanned her notes and read, "A 'sacrifice' means offering something in pursuit of a higher aim, such as the advancement of knowledge."

"Thank you, Mel. The rest of you, please copy that definition into your notes and be prepared for a quiz on the termination process tomorrow."

As they went about their assignment, Mrs. Mendall's sixth-graders seemed to forget the figure in the CM2029. Only one student watched as the glass, once fogged by the breath of curious students, steamed from the inside as its occupant expired on the altar of education. The heat lamps warmed their subject in vain as the heart rate monitor flatlined silently.

"Work on your notes, Jane," said Mrs. Mendall wearily.

Jane nodded but made no move to grasp her tablet and stylus.

"Are you sure you're up to being back so soon? I know you and Bethany were close."

Jane nodded again.

"How was the funeral?"

"It was nice," said Jane. "They read something I thought was interesting — something about 'you knit me together in my mother's womb.' It sounded nice." Mrs. Mendall said nothing. She knew the passage.

Within the Class Mother 2029, the sacrifice stiffened and grew no more. Its expansion into a recognizable lifeform had taken most of the year; its demise had occurred in seconds. Mrs. Mendall did her best not to dwell on this pitiful ratio of life to death as she watched her students depart. She gathered her things, emptying her mind as, soon, she would empty the incubator. Resolutely, she reached for the CM2029's power switch.

It was finished.

The next day, the sacrifice was gone. No yellow shirts were worn in its memory. No side-by-side photographs documented its development. After a frenzy of dissections and lab write-ups, a final bell released Mrs. Mendall's students for summer vacation. As their shouts and laughter faded, she returned to her desk. For the last time, she withdrew the old photo in its frame and, with a single, practiced movement, tossed it into the wastebasket: another bitter, empty cup.

Ryanne Molinari is a pianist/organist based in Cedar Rapids, Iowa. She received her Bachelor of Music from Biola University, where she was a member of the Torrey Honors College. Ryanne continued to earn her Master of Letters in Theology and the Arts from the University of St. Andrews, Scotland, focusing on musical practice as a spiritual discipline, and she is currently pursuing her Doctor of Ministry from Covenant Theological Seminary.

To read/listen to more of Ryanne's work, follow her on Instagram @Ryanne_JM or check out her website: RyanneMolinari.com.

Amy Willoughby-Burle

Jesus Drives a '65 Mustang

Arthur stands outside the hospital chapel, looking in but not stepping forward. Arthur wants to want to go in, but he can't seem to make himself do it. Jesus knows that Arthur isn't actually going to go into the dismal cavern of the hospital chapel. No one likes it in there, least of all Jesus. It's dark and smells like the inside of a teenage boy's Converse sneaker.

Arthur goes instead to the cafeteria. The aroma of meatloaf with brown gravy isn't too much better, but at least there are windows. At least there is light.

Jesus sits at a table by the door. He gets a lot of double takes from people on their way out, but most of the time folks just chuckle to themselves and keep going. No one even stops to ask if it's really him, like they would if they thought he was Henry Cavill. But then you'd be talking about Superman, and Jesus doesn't want to ponder whether or not people think that he or Superman would come out ahead in a battle for supreme power. He knows the answer to that, but he's sure most people don't agree with him these days.

Jesus knows Arthur is on the fence about that too, and Jesus really needs to speak with him, but Arthur's daughter Sharon has him engaged for the moment.

"Jesus drives an old Mustang?" Sharon asks, repeating in question the ridiculous statement her father just made. She's somewhat exasperated, but mostly just exhausted. Not with her father—with the situation they're both in.

"Why wouldn't he?" Arthur says to his grown daughter as they sit in the hospital cafeteria, while his other child, Andy, is upstairs waiting to die just before his thirty-seventh birthday. "Jesus is retro. He's old school."

"You don't think Jesus would want power locks and windows," Arthur's daughter asks, pushing an escaped pea across the table with her fork.

Arthur holds his hands up and out in front of him. "Behold I say, unlock. And it is unlocked."

Jesus chuckles. People think he's so serious, but that doesn't mean

112

he doesn't like a good laugh. His father invented laughter after all. And Arthur's funny, he really is, but Sharon doesn't laugh. Andy would laugh. He has a great sense of humor. When you're doomed from the start, you have to find a way to make life bearable. Laughter helps.

There's no way out of this that leaves Andy alive and Arthur doesn't know how he's going to talk about his son in the past tense. How do fathers talk about their sons like that? He was supposed to be able to tell people about Andy's new job, his fiancé, the wedding, their new baby, the two-story house in the suburbs. That's what the other men on the golf course talk about. Andy had a fiancé, but she'd left a while back when things got really wonky. Even here at the end, Andy had almost rallied, but then suffered a blood pressure crash and then spike that put him into a semi-coma and pretty much fried his brain. No one wants to hear about that on the 9th hole. No one wants to watch a grown man cry.

Jesus and Andy have something in common. Andy doesn't mean to make his father sad, but it's just the way this one is meant to go. If Arthur could turn the daytime sky black and send a noise so loud it shook the earth, he'd do it, just like God did. All fathers would—the ones who watch their sons stop breathing.

Jesus sighs.

Andy was born with the cards stacked against him, but a parent has to hope for the best. They have to. Knowing something is inevitable doesn't make it any easier—you can ask the Big Guy about that one. Arthur already hates that people will temper his grief for him by pointing out that his son had been sick for so long and *really, isn't it better now that he's out of pain*. He'll probably even say that too, which really pisses him off because all he really wants to do is cry and punch someone in the face.

Arthur has been in and out of the hospital with Andy over the years, and most of the time they jokingly referred to it as routine maintenance—to be expected with cases like his. They'd done the Holiday in the Hospital too many times to count. Andy had summered on the seventh floor. They referred to it as their second home in the city. Andy had beaten the odds before, but there's no coming back from this one.

Arthur knows it. He meant to go to the chapel while the nurses did their assessing and charting, but he'd ended up in the cafeteria instead. No matter, he thought. Jesus could just as easily be in the cafeteria if he was anywhere at all. He assumed the chapel would be empty, but in the cafeteria he wouldn't be alone. Arthur had sat a long while before his daughter found him. He wasn't sure how they had come to the topic of what Jesus would drive. Arthur figures people ponder a lot of things about Jesus while they wait in the hospital.

But they probably don't expect to run into him in the elevator or pass him in the halls. Jesus wishes people would at least look for him. When someone does notice him, they mostly just stop him for directions, which he's happy to give. Actually, Sharon had asked him where the cafeteria was when she'd come looking for Arthur.

"Right in front of you," Jesus had said and pointed to the windowed doors they were both headed toward.

Sharon had nodded and had gone in ahead of him.

"You don't think he'd want something newer?" Sharon asks now about the car, stabbing the pea and depositing it back on her plate. "Something to show he's up with the times."

Sharon had found Arthur sitting at a table, tearing up a napkin to no reasonable avail. She'd gotten a tray of food for each of them, but neither could think of eating. Arthur appreciates the gesture though. Ritual is supposed to be comforting.

"That's just the thing," Arthur says and pointlessly shakes salt over the thick, brown, beef-like substance on his tray. "Jesus doesn't need a Lincoln Navigator with Bluetooth capabilities and a GPS."

Sharon drives a Lincoln Navigator with Bluetooth capabilities and a GPS. Arthur sees his daughter wince, and he feels bad. He didn't mean to make some sort of comparison. It was just the first vehicle he could think of. He knows she will read things into his statement and get upset about something that he didn't even mean. But years of failed attempts at explaining himself, only to make the situation worse, keep his mouth closed around the words he wishes he could say. Arthur peeks at Sharon, when she's not looking, to see if he can gauge anything. For the moment, she seems to let the car comment slide. Impending grief has been good therapy for them in the past. When Arthur's wife died, he and Sharon and Andy had clung to all the good parts of their relationships for quite a while. Arthur likes feeling closer to his daughter now, but the trade off will most likely be the death of him.

"I don't know," Sharon says and sighs. "There are a few more streets out here than there were back in the day. Stop lights and Starbucks, and even the Lord could get distracted and miss his turn off."

Arthur thinks about Jesus pulling off onto the shoulder of the road, opening up the map, and trying to figure out how he got lost. Perhaps Jesus would see the fluorescents from outside and come into the cafeteria for a bite to eat. Arthur thinks about the hospital cafeteria as a holding tank—the real waiting room, where everyone is lost. Better than the chapel maybe. More tangible in a situation like this.

Maybe Jesus prefers the cafeteria too, Arthur thinks. Arthur imagines Jesus, man of the people, eating at one of the wobbly, wooden tables night after night. Folks praying so hard he can't get a moment to eat his banana pudding. Would anyone blame him if he spent too much money on a vintage convertible and hit the road? Arthur sighs, and Sharon reaches across the table, putting her hand over his. He's so desperate for her touch that it burns just a little.

"Do you use your GPS?" Arthur asks, pulling his hand out from under Sharon's even though he wants to grip it tight. "Doesn't anyone know how to read a map anymore?"

"Dad?" Sharon says, but doesn't finish whatever she was going to say.

Arthur's car has a GPS too, but he doesn't use it. He can't stand the sound of the GPS's voice. It's so sure about everything. Even when it's wrong.

"No," Sharon admits with a glint of relief in her smile. "That voice makes me crazy."

Arthur smiles too. Just for a second.

"Jesus doesn't need that lady, anyway," Arthur says and then affects the cadence of the GPS voice. "Jesus already knows to '*turn right at the next intersection*.' He doesn't need to be told he has '*arrived at his destination*'."

"Dad," Sharon says softly, the tears Arthur has dreaded finally coming in. "Does it really matter what Jesus would drive?"

Arthur is sick of the fluorescent lights of the cafeteria and wants to step outside into the darkness of one, last, simple evening. But that evening is gone already; it passed without him noticing it.

"Sure it matters," Arthur says, getting a little indignant for reasons he's not even sure of. "Jesus didn't have much competition for people's attention back then. Now, it's a whole different show. Back then, being the dude who could raise the dead had some cache," he says. "Cure a leper—pretty impressive. Heal the blind—not a bad trick. But now-a-days, a good doctor and a bottle of pills can pretty much do all that."

If only, Arthur thinks. But miracles are still God's to do and if he did them all the time, it wouldn't be the same. Arthur likens it to the way people don't listen to Christmas music all year 'round. Or shoot off fireworks every weekend. Arthur knows all this, but still.

He looks at the clock on the cafeteria wall and then closes his eyes. Tomorrow at 11:00am. That's as long as they're giving Andy to miraculously come through. *"It shouldn't take long,"* the nurse had said about the process of letting Andy die. The nurse was young, and her haircut told Arthur she didn't have kids. No one with kids has time for hair like that. Arthur knew the girl had meant it as a comfort. He didn't expect her to realize that losing his son would take the rest of Arthur's life. It wasn't about the time it took to pull tubes out and turn things off.

"We should get back upstairs," Sharon says, looking at her phone, checking the time.

Arthur hates the way nothing is like he remembers it. What had been so wrong with a wristwatch? How had everything changed so drastically in the last thirty-some years? Thirty years is a long time, Arthur figures, but it doesn't sound so long when it's the measure of a child's life. His child's life.

Sharon starts to stand up, but Arthur clears his throat and she sits back down.

"Anyway, Jesus has to stand out when he rolls by you," Arthur says, gesturing too widely with his hands, not ready to go back upstairs. "He wants you to see him. He wants you to aim your smartphone at him and video him for YouTube."

Jesus on YouTube? Has it come to that? Jesus shakes his head; he hopes not. But Arthur can understand it—the desire to be seen in this whacked-out world of nonsense. He imagines Jesus in his '65 red convertible with the top down. He's got his arm resting on the window rim, his dark hair blowing around in the rushing wind, his olive skin soaking up the sun. He gives a nod when you pass by. Your mouth falls open and you nudge your passenger to *"look dude, there goes Jesus."*

"Where, man? I didn't see him," your passenger says.

"Typical," Jesus laments, because he can hear the conversation in the other car. He can hear all the conversations in all the cars.

He can hear Arthur, too—even when he doesn't say anything. That's the beauty part—if people would just see it.

Maybe Jesus will pull in at Starbucks and order a vanilla latte, he thinks. He's interested in seeing how Arthur's daydream of him plays out. Why not? He hears people talking about the place all the time. *Jesus, Starbucks coffee is expensive.*

Inside, his coffee costs the better part of a five, which he manifests out of his pocket. He gets a kick out of seeing "Jesus" written in Sharpie on the side of the cup—quotation marks and all. Outside, there are no tables empty, so Jesus has to beg for a spot at someone else's.

"Story of my life," he says and sits down with a longhaired hippie.

The hippie tells Jesus he's trying to build a chicken coop.

"I can help with that, man," Jesus says.

He can almost feel the weight of the hammer in his hand and the metallic ting of the nails held tight in his teeth while he works. But then he remembers with a shudder why he hasn't gone back to carpentry. Wood and nails aren't the same anymore.

"So you in, dude?" the hippie asks.

Jesus shrugs and tosses his empty cup into the trash. As he and the hippie walk through the parking lot, Jesus glances at the Mustang. He was on his way somewhere, wasn't he? He just meant to stop off for a caffeine buzz and then get back on the road.

But what's the point? No one even knows he's here.

At the hippie's house, someone hands Jesus a hammer. It's a bit lighter than he thought it would be—fiberglass handle perhaps. He's impressed. There's a pile of lumber scraps that Jesus figures is meant to be the coop. He pulls a couple of large beams loose and grabs some nails. He means to make a chicken coop—really he does. But he fashions a cross instead. He can't help himself. He rests it on his shoulder and turns back toward the highway.

"Dude," the hippie calls out to him.

Jesus raises one hand in a wave without looking back. He makes it through traffic to the Mustang and ties the cross to the top of the car. At least the trip will be easier on his back this time. Jesus pulls slowly into traffic, taking care with the cross. People honk and give him the finger. He doesn't take it personally. They've got free will after all.

While he's driving, Jesus thinks about Arthur and his son in the ICU on the fourth floor. Time to get back to it. He wants to tell Arthur to go ahead and pray as much as he wants to, that he doesn't like banana pudding anyway.

Jesus ignores the no parking signs and leaves the Mustang by the door. He goes up to the fourth floor and sits with Arthur and Sharon and Andy through the night and into the last day until Andy has left the building with a smile and nod at Jesus as he heads on home.

Outside the hospital, after Sharon and Arthur have said their goodbyes for a moment, so that Sharon can check in on her family and Arthur can do whatever it is he's supposed to do now, Jesus steps up beside him and points at the car.

"Nice ride, huh?" Jesus says.

Arthur looks at him and then looks again at the '65 Mustang, his mouth dropping open just a tad.

"Hop in," Jesus says now that this part is over and the rest is yet to come. "Let's tool around town for a while? If you don't mind my company."

"I could use it," Arthur says, and they get into the car and drive away. "Was it worth it?" Arthur asks once they're out on the highway and headed into everything that comes next.

Jesus looks over at Arthur and smiles. Arthur nods and says, "Yeah, it was worth it for me too. Even though it didn't turn out like I wanted it to."

Jesus knows how bad this part will hurt. But just like Arthur, Jesus knows that if he had to do it all over again, he still would.

Amy Willoughby-Burle is a writer and teacher living in the mountains near Asheville, North Carolina, with her husband and five children. She is the author of three novels, *The Other Side of Certain, The Lemonade Year*, and *The Year of Thorns and Honey*, as well as one short story collection titled *Out Across the Nowhere*. God is present in her fiction, and she hopes people will see Him there and perhaps want to take the time to get to know Him better.

HOMILIES

Douglas J. Lindquist

Seeking the God Who Hides

I'd like to address a question that has puzzled God's people for thousands of years. The basic issue can be put like this: why isn't God more obvious? As believers, we know that God has revealed himself in Jesus, but most of us still have moments where we wonder. We wonder where God is when we suffer. We wonder why God doesn't appear in all his glory for every believer to see. We wonder why God seems to work in ways that are subtle and quiet.

The Bible describes God as hidden. It comes as a surprise to many people that the God of Scripture does not reveal himself to the full extent that he could. He could have decided to constantly make his presence plain to all Christians. He could have made himself as obvious as the physical world. He could have sent Jesus to personally appear to each one of his followers, but he did not.

This work focuses on three parts of this challenge. First, we will see what Scripture says about God's hiddenness. Secondly, we will try to understand why God has chosen to hide. Finally, I will suggest some ways we can find a deeper relationship with our hidden God.

Most Christians know from experience that sometimes God seems hidden. Of course, the Bible also shows certain moments when God is unusually close to people or when he opens up the heavens for them. For the prophet Ezekiel, "the heavens were opened and I saw visions of God" (1:1). Stephen, the first martyr of the church, cried out while he was being killed, "'I see heaven open and the Son of Man standing at the right hand of God'" (Acts 7:56). The Apostle Paul "was caught up to paradise. He heard inexpressible things, things that man is not permitted to tell" (2 Cor. 12:4). But these moments are rare.

Eventually all Christians will see God face-to-face, and that will be the most beautiful experience imaginable. But not yet. We currently live in a time where God is not so obvious. The Scriptures portray the pain of life with a Lord who seems distant. The Psalmist shouts: "How long, O Lord? Will you forget me forever? How long will you hide your face from me?" (13:1), "Why do you hide your face and forget our affliction and our oppression?" (44:24), "Why do you stand afar off, O Lord? Why do you hide yourself in times of trouble?" (10:1), "Give ear to my prayer, O God; And do not hide yourself from my supplication" (55:1). Even Jesus felt abandoned by the Father when he suffered on the cross (Matt. 27:46).

The Son of God came to earth in a subtle and secret way. He didn't come as a great earthly ruler or military figure. He didn't come in great wealth or fame. He came in the humblest of circumstances. In Luke's Gospel, angels appear to unassuming shepherds to announce the coming Savior and Lord. They tell them that the long-awaited Messiah that Israel had expected for centuries would come as "'a baby wrapped in swaddling cloths and lying in a manger'" (2:12). Then, as Jesus grew up, he experienced thirty years away from the spotlight, living an ordinary life and not calling attention to who he was until three years before his death. Paul tells us that Jesus: "Who, being in very nature God, did not consider equality with God something to be used to his own advantage; rather, he made himself nothing by taking the very nature of a servant, being made in human likeness. And being found in appearance as a man, he humbled himself by becoming obedient to death— even death on a cross" (Phil. 2:6–8). In this way, Jesus hid his identity for most of his life. We see a glimpse of his true glory at the transfiguration, when he was with Peter, James, and John, and "his face shone like the sun, and his clothes became as white as the light" (Matt. 17:2). But only a glimpse. For the present time, as Isaiah concluded long ago, "Truly," the Lord is a "God who hides himself" (45:15).

The Bible is clear that God hides, but why does he do it? Why doesn't he overwhelm us with his presence all the time? To answer this question, we need to look at Genesis chapter three. After Adam and Eve rebelled against God and brought shame into their lives, verse eight tells us that "then the man and his wife heard the sound of the Lord God as he was walking in the garden in the cool of the day, and they hid from the Lord God among the trees of the garden." At first glance it seems bizarre that humans would try to hide from God, since God is present everywhere. But what this passage implies is that while God *is* everywhere, he does not make his presence *felt* everywhere. While God was not pleased that Adam and Eve disobeyed, he knew that they would want to hide from him, so he hid his being to some degree from them. The story reveals this fact: if God were to always make his presence felt everywhere, people would not be free to turn from him. God respects the freedom of human beings so much that he hides to allow us to hide from him. He has set up human history so that those who refuse his love and grace don't have to accept him. Those who want to avoid his presence can, at least for now.

God also hides from believers when we rebel against his desires. Isaiah explains: "Surely the arm of the Lord is not too short to save nor his ear too dull to hear. But your iniquities have separated you from your God; your sins have hidden his face from you, so that he will not hear" (59:1–2). Indeed, this was the frequent sin of Israel and one of the reasons Jesus was not more obvious about his mission. Jesus was asked why he spoke of the kingdom of God using parables, and quoting Isaiah, he responded: "'For this people's heart has become calloused; they hardly hear with their ears, and they have closed their eyes'" (Matt. 13:15). It is not the case that God first hardened Israel and wanted to keep them from salvation, but rather, Israel chose spiritual blindness and deafness, and Jesus was respecting their choice. The message of Scripture is that God can reach a point where he gives people over to their desires and he allows them to suffer the consequences (Rom. 1).

We shouldn't think that God hides himself out of cruelty, since the story of Scripture makes it clear that God desires a relationship with all people. God is "not wanting anyone to perish, but everyone to come to repentance" (2 Pet. 3:9). God "desires all people to be saved and to come to the knowledge of the truth" (1 Tim. 2:4). God hides because he respects us. He does not want to force himself on us. Have you ever known someone who does not respect your space and is constantly trying to force his presence on you? It is not a pleasant experience. God is a gentleman who woos us, not an intruder who barges in on us.

God could have easily chosen to make human beings like robots. He could have designed us to automatically say "I love you, God." But that's not true friendship. Friendship requires both sides to freely choose to spend time with each other. It cannot be forced. *The biggest reason God hides is because he wants us to choose to seek him.* Moses reminds us that "you will seek the Lord your God and you will find him, if you search after him with all your heart and with all your soul" (Deut. 4:29). The Psalmist declares: "The young lions suffer want and hunger; but those who seek the Lord lack no good thing" (34:10). James encourages us to "draw near to God, and he will draw near to you" (4:8). Jesus joins this chorus: "'Ask, and it will be given to you; seek, and you will find; knock, and it will be opened to you'"

(Matt. 7:7).

God has ordered human history so that all who want his presence get it, all who seek him find him, all who have eyes to see and ears to hear will be granted a relationship with him. Paul knew that when God made people, he "'determined allotted periods and the boundaries of their dwelling place, that they should seek God, in the hope that they might feel their way toward him and find him. Yet he is actually not far from each one of us'" (Acts 17:26-27).

It is comforting to know that God wants us to seek him, but how do we go about it? Let me mention three things. First, we can learn to practice the presence of God. An easy way to do this is to pause for thirty seconds several times a day and ask Jesus to fill you with peace or tell him what worries and cares are on your mind. Another way to do this is to take short walks and focus your thoughts on the Lord. In these ways we can learn to pray continually as Paul suggests (1 Thess. 5:17).

Secondly, we know we are saved by grace and that God accepts us based on Christ's righteousness. We also know we still sin. A good practice to help with this is to keep a short account with God. This means that whenever we make a mistake, as soon as we realize what we've done, we can tell God we are sorry and strive to do better from then on. While we are not saved by our moral performance, we still need to repent and confess our sins to maintain a strong connection to the Lord (1 John 1:9).

A final practice that will help is to daily meditate on key Bible passages. We don't need to read huge portions, but we can select certain encouraging sections of Scripture and ponder them in our hearts over and over. Great texts for this are Psalm 23, Colossians 3, Romans 8, John 3 and Philippians 2–4, among others. God's presence often flows through passages like these.

Douglas J. Lindquist is Content Editor and Theology Editor of Solum Press. He graduated from New Hope Christian College with a BA in Ministry Leadership and from Talbot School of Theology with an MA in Philosophy. His academic writing has appeared in the _Journal of Contemporary Theological Studies._ He currently teaches philosophy at Grand Canyon University.

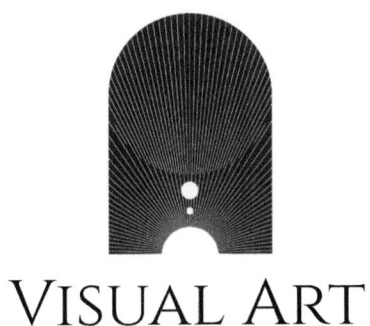

VISUAL ART

GJ GILLESPIE

Gillespie, *The Lionhearted Man*, 2023. Collage.

Gillespie, *The Man Who Fell to Earth*, 2023. Collage.

Gillespie, *Temptation of St. Anthony*, 2023. Collage.

GJ Gillespie is a collage artist living in a 1928 Tudor Revival farmhouse overlooking Oak Harbor on Whidbey Island (north of Seattle). In addition to natural beauty, he is inspired by art history — especially midcentury abstract expressionism. The "Northwest Mystics" who produced haunting images from this region 60 years ago are favorites. Winner of 20 awards, his art has appeared in 61 shows and 100 publications. When he is not making art, he runs his sketchbook company Leda Art Supply.

ZACH MOLL

Moll, *Snow IV,* 2023. Acrylic, Clay, and Leaves.

Zach Moll is a painter from Nebraska. He has degrees in Graphic Design and Studio Art from Concordia University, NE. He is the Art Director of Vanora, an artist collaboration project that he co-founded in 2019. Zach spent time as a liturgical artist at the Center for Liturgical Art, a studio specializing in artwork, stained glass, and furnishings for the Church. Zach's art practice revolves around the interplay of shape and color, the physicality of raw materials, and the agency a painting can contain.

Cynthia Yatchman

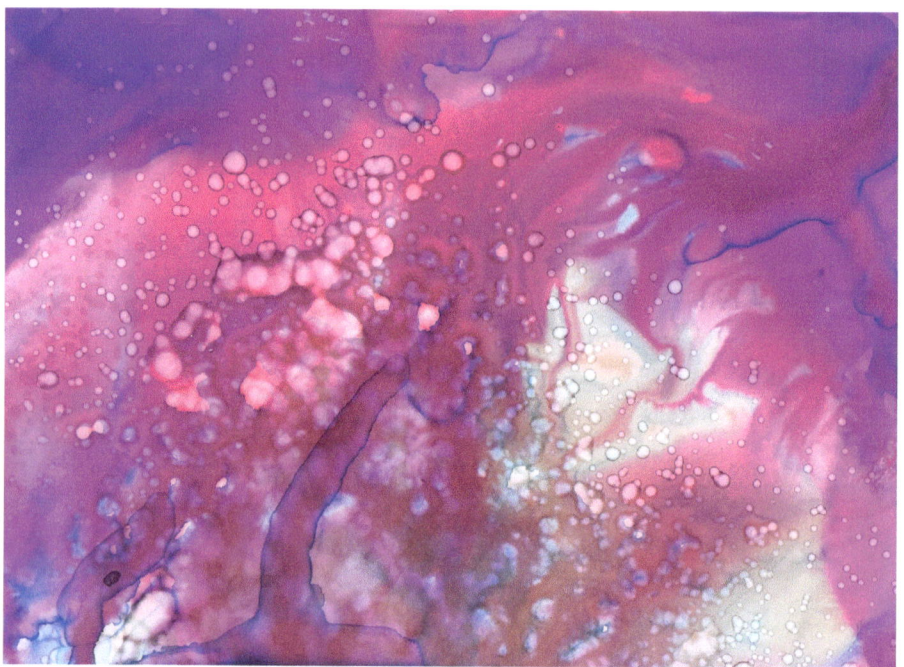

Yatchman, *COVID Color,* 2023.

Cynthia Yatchman is a Seattle-based artist and art instructor. With an M.A. in child development and a B. A. in education, she has a strong interest in art education and teaches art to adults, children and families in Seattle. As a former ceramicist, she studied with J.T. Abernathy in Ann Arbor, MI. However, after receiving her B.F.A. in painting from the University of Washington, she switched from 3D art to 2D and has remained there ever since. She works primarily on paintings, prints and collages. Her art is housed in numerous public and private collections and she has been shown nationally in California, Connecticut, New York, Indiana, Michigan, Oregon and Wyoming. She has exhibited extensively in the Northwest, including shows at Seattle University, Seattle Pacific University, Shoreline Community College, the Tacoma and Seattle Convention Centers, and the Pacific Science Center. She is a member of the Seattle Print Art Association, COCA (Center of Contemporary Art) and the Puget Sound Painters.

www.ingramcontent.com/pod-product-compliance
Lightning Source LLC
Chambersburg PA
CBHW041412010726
47507CB00005B/251